EMOTIONAL CHAOS

Brian Codagnone

Penhallow
Publishing

EMOTIONAL CHAOS

Published by
Penhallow Publishing

International Standard (ISBN) # 978-0-9776375-1-5

Library of Congress Control Number: 2012912413

Printed in the USA

First Printing 2012

"Humor is emotional chaos remembered in tranquility."
- James Thurber

Emotional Chaos

IS THAT YOUR AURA
OR ARE YOU JUST HAPPY TO SEE ME?

While the desire to communicate with the dead has been around since ancient times (the Greek scholar Eucalyptus frequently had conversations with his long dead brother. His brother was still in the room at the time and not getting any fresher, so the authorities finally had to step in), most scholars believe that the modern Spiritualism Movement began with the Fox sisters of Hydesville, New York. In 1848 the girls claimed to hear "strange, rapping sounds" in the night. As it was a slow news decade, they soon attracted a wide following. The clairvoyant Andrew Jackson Davis took it a step further. While in a trance he foresaw the coming of the spiritualist movement, which is rather like your contractor foreseeing that you're going to be paying for his new boat. Even the citizens of Hydesville wouldn't fall for that one. Although the Fox sisters later confessed to fraud, the Spiritualism Movement swept the nation. There were so many psychics, mediums and clairvoyants around that in order to get noticed, you needed a really good hook.

The era saw the appearance of such personalities as The Flamenco Dancing Prophet, The Spoon Playing Seer, The All-Seeing Oculist, Tourette Syndrome Tommy, Count "Count the Spoons" Orlov, Hornblowing Horatio, The Finder of Lost Luggage, and The Cat Slammer Kid. Later came Hersey Waddell, known as "The Nostradamus of the Tri-Cities Area". In 1929 he made the shocking prediction that "A major Wall Street figure will get a splinter, and it will become infected". Many later felt that this foretold the devastating Wall Street Crash, but it was discovered that he meant it literally. In October of that year J. Waldo Bismark, head of the prestigious brokerage house of Bismark, Ringworm and Sheepshank, did indeed get a splinter, and a painful one at that.

Some of the most famous psychics of the time included:

Emotional Chaos

Hercules Biggerstaff, the world's strongest tarot card reader. Biggerstaff was able to bench press any client while reading their fate in the cards. Often he would bend iron bars to impress clients who were unhappy with their fortunes or just reluctant to pay.

Madam Domino, who promised to read your future in thirty minutes or less, or your reading was free. Often, to build suspense, she would wait twenty eight or twenty nine minutes and then blurt out the client's fortune. Most customers soon realized that it was a gimmick, but they got free breadsticks, so few complained.

Maurice La Merde, the Penalty Box Prophet, took advantage of the superstition of hockey players in the early days of the NHL. La Merde would walk through the locker room and "read the aura" of the players, predicting who would get penalties and who wouldn't. He gained fame in 1933 with his uncannily accurate prediction that Montreal Canadiens star Aurel Joliat would get "two minutes for tripping" in the second period of a bout between the Canadiens and the arch-rival Maple Leafs. His reputation suffered somewhat when he failed to predict the rash of penalties that led to a 10-0 drubbing by the Boston Bruins, but came back when he predicted the famous penalty shot by Teeder Kennedy on Bill Durnan (the actual prediction was "a man in blue shall be wronged, and wreak his vengeance on a man in red", which, since it was a Toronto-Montreal game seemed like a pretty safe bet, but it was a simpler time and people were more trusting). His downfall came abruptly in 1943 when he was caught "reading the aura" of the stick boy in equipment room. Plus, he confessed that he was making predictions for the sole reason of seeing games for free.

The Fortune Cookie Reader would go with his clients to Chinese restaurants and read their fortune cookies for them. Why anyone would pay for that is still a mystery.

The Wildly Inaccurate Millicent, who prided herself that her predictions were never right. Being the jazz age, when pleasure reigned and the public craved the novel and the absurd, people flocked to her door to hear such predictions as "You will soon be elected President of Luxembourg", (even though every schoolboy knew that Luxembourg was a constitutional monarchy), or "I see you eating seven hams in the near future", even though the client, Rabbi Chaim Braunstein, was well known to keep kosher. When the stock market crashed people no longer had time for such frivolity and Millicent faded from the scene. Her fifteen minutes of fame had expired, but ironically, her last public prediction that "Someday a man named Andy Warhol will coin the phrase 'in the future everyone will be famous for fifteen minutes' " turned out to be uncannily accurate.

The Screaming Prophet of Doom, who was not just inaccurate, but really annoying.

DEATH OF THE BLUES

For the musician, there seems to be almost a romance in dying young. For some, like Buddy Holly, it comes too soon. For some, like Elvis, it comes too late. Still, dying young is often a good career move. Can any of us imagine a seventy year old Jim Morrison? Janis Joplin appearing as a judge on *American Idol*, or Jimi Hendrix doing a guest shot on *Will and Grace*?

This was especially true with The Blues. It could have been the times in which they lived and the world that shaped them; poverty, segregation, Jim Crow, the hard life and temptations of the road, the torment of genius. But who can forget the legacy they left, unforgettable songs such as "I May be Color Blind but I Know I Got the Blues", "Scorned Woman With A Chain Saw", "Broken Face Blues", "I Headed for Memphis but Ended up in Hell", "The Last Train to Chattanooga Done Run Over my Dog" and "Forcin' A Frenchman Down a Hole Blues" (which was banned in Alabama for being both "immoral and obtuse")? But, as the old saying goes, you have to suffer to sing the blues.

One of the last surviving musicians of the Golden Age of the Blues is Duncan "Cake" Hines. Best known for the classic songs "Belly Full of Buckshot Blues", "Fixin' to Hemorrhage", "Groin Injury Blues (My Woman Kicked Me Hard)" and, of course, "My Woman's Like A Chicken Bone in My Throat", Hines played with the likes of Professor Longhair, Big Mama Thornton, T-Bone Walker, Son House and Willie Brown. Still performing despite being 89 years old, we spoke to the blues legend when he was playing a gig at a local jazz club with the great Blind Jellyroll Berkowitz ("I Got Two Glass Eyes But Still I See (How My Baby Been Cheating on Me")", "Downed Power Line on a Wet Road Blues", etc). We found him to be enthusiastic, passionate about his music and unfortunately, mad as a hatter. He was philosophical about the life of a bluesman.

Emotional Chaos

"Sure, some of us lived to be old men; Lightnin' Hopkins, Muddy Waters, B. B. King, T-Bone Walker, but we're rarer than albinos in politics. So many died too young. Just look at Robert Johnson, Blind Lemon Jefferson, Blind Willie Johnson. A lotta blindness, too, now that I think about it. Yes, sir. A whole lotta blindness..."

He leaned over and took a sip out of the Coleman lantern that stood on a table near his beloved guitar "Kierkegaard", the only instrument he'd played in his seventy-plus year career. "Lotta tragedy, too. It was a hard life. Look at Leadbelly, Tommy Johnson, Memphis Sadie, Big Papa Poe, Broken Neck Parker, Otis 'High Cholesterol' Rupp, Elmore 'Night Terrors' Brown, Bessie 'Convulsing Molly' Doak, Bowel Obstruction Benson, Torn Rotator Cuff Coleman, Violent Mood Swings Turner... I remember my first side man, 'Harpoon Through The Eye' Harper. He got that nickname doin' a stretch in Joliet for bein' a heroin addict. Funny story, but anyway, Harpoon Through the Eye died young, too. He got hit by a bus crossin' the street in Jackson, Mississippi. Bad depth perception. Sad, really sad."

He seemed to brighten a little when he noticed us looking at his famous guitar. It was worn with age, but looked smooth, mellow, the very soul of the blues. "You see this guitar? Willie 'Bipolar' Jefferson wrote 'Big Hot Mamma's Got a Small Cold Heart' on this very guitar. It was about Bertha 'Sassy Mama' Buell, the singer Bessie Smith herself called, "The best woman blues singer since Lulu 'Repetitive Strain Injury' Coolidge". I can't think of higher praise than that, can you? He gave it to me just before he died of the gum disease known as gingivitis. Yes, sir, if this guitar could talk..."

He caressed the guitar like an oddly shaped woman and took another drink. "Like I said, it was a hard life. You probably don't remember Lester 'Inflamed Lymph Nodes' Boone. When he wrote 'There Ain't Enough Whiskey in Tennessee to Wash my Blues Away', he was being literal. They found him in a barrel at the Jack

Emotional Chaos

Daniels distillery. It was his request that they bury him in that barrel, which is good, 'cause it would be distressin' to be sippin' whiskey in a bar some night and find a cufflink in it."

It was finally time for him to take the stage and do what he had been doing for the better part of the 20th century, what he did best. He only stopped long enough to drop a bowling ball on his foot. "Like they say", he said with a wink, "You gotta suffer to play the blues!"

A DEUCED AFFAIR AT ROTTING MOLARS

An Inspector Blancmange Mystery

Ever since Sherlock Holmes was created in the 19th century, British detective fiction has been popular the world over. Whether set in the foggy London of Jack the Ripper, the bleak and forbidding moors or a remote manor house in the country, readers have gotten to study the suspects, sort out the red herrings and try to solve the crime before the detective gathered everyone into the sitting room to expose the truth, no matter how sordid. Of course, Sherlock Holmes was the most famous, but he was by no means the only sleuth in Victorian England. The brilliant detective is as much a part of English life as tea and strangely named food.

A lesser known detective of the era was the great Inspector Blancmange. Blancmange, the son of a British mother and French father was always viewed with skepticism by Scotland Yard (a common bigotry at the time. When cases hit a dead end, the Metropolitan Police were known to round up the usual immigrants, drifters, Jews and Frenchmen. Being French, they usually broke first under the rubber hose, solving many a case). Inspector Blancmange was assisted in his work by his friend and biographer, Colonel Sebastian Broadbeam, late of the Royal Horse Marines. The first Inspector Blancmange story, "The Curious Case of the Shriveled Grape" appeared in the Strand Magazine on September 4, 1892. It was quickly followed by "The Spoon Collector's Plight" (Rousing Tales, December 12, 1892) and "The Railwayman's Spleen" (The Times of London, February 20, 1893). His most famous case, "A Deuced Affair at Rotting Molars", set the standard for British country house murder mysteries. Who can forget the cast of players: Wattery Graves, a bounder; Boris Wrackingkov, a White Russian expatriate; Fauldeed, an Arab; Lady Penelope, a dowager with a past; Gwendolyn, the daughter of the house; Hatchett, the butler and, of course, Lord Bevis Ashenhyde, Fifth Earl of Foetid, Sussex. The story begins at the remote estate of Rotting Molars, ancestral seat of the Earls of Foetid. It's a weekend of shooting, only no one suspects that more than the grouse will taste buckshot before the day is done. We join the scene at dinner:

Lady Penelope: "Has anyone seen Lord Bevis? His Spotted Dick is getting quite cold!"

Hatchett: "I'll look in the library. I heard gunshots from that direction, perhaps he's shooting some servants again."

Graves: "Serves the buggers right, being lower class!"

Gwendolyn: "Oh, don't be like that! Without the serving class who'd clean the grouse?"

Lady Penelope: "The house?"

Wrackingkov: "I believe she said 'grouse', madam."

Hatchett: "If I may interrupt. Lord Bevis is dead. Shot. Rather messily, I might add."

Everyone: "I say!"

The local constabulary, being as thick as a cast iron condom, call in Scotland Yard. Not being much better at it, but not being stupid either, the Yard calls in the man who's solved all their cases, Inspector Blancmange. Blancmange and Broadbeam round up the usual suspects in the library:

Blancmange: "One of you in this room murdered Lord Bevis!"

Broadbeam: "I hope you don't suspect me, Blancmange!"

Blancmange: "Sit down, you idiot. As I was saying, Lord Bevis is dead, and one of you did it!"

Graves: "Fauldeed's a foreigner and a wog to boot! I say he did it!"

Fauldeed: "I couldn't have done it! My trigger finger was maimed

Emotional Chaos

in the service of the Sultan of Turkey! I have no reason to wish Lord Bevis dead! Besides, Wrackingkov is a foreigner, too!"

Lady Penelope: "A conspiracy!"

Blancmange: "Are you done? Can we get on with this?"

Gwendolyn: "So sorry, Inspector, but you know what murder does to one!"

Blancmange: "All too well, miss. Now, as I was saying, the only one of you who had means, motive and opportunity is... Hatchett, the butler!"

Everyone (except Hatchett): "I say!"

Hatchett: "Even though you have no evidence whatsoever, I'll admit I did it! I'm glad I did it! He was a rotter! A right rotter!"

Blancmange: "Well, that solves that."

Gwendolyn: "Good show! Tea and bangers anyone?"

And, for the first time in detective fiction, the butler did it. Of course, over the years it would become a cliche, but for Inspector Blancmange, the immortal detective that Sir Arthur Conan Doyle himself called "A cheap ripoff of Sherlock Holmes. You'll be hearing from my solicitors", it was still original, so it was a brilliant piece of deduction. Or a lucky guess.

CURIOUS TALES OF
OLD NEW ENGLAND

Hysteria in Salem

We all know the story of the Salem Witch Trials, but how many have heard of the story of Hormel Thatcher? A full ten years before witch hysteria gripped Salem Village, Thatcher lived with his wife Misery, his daughters Dorcas, Submit and Infection and his sons Groininjury and Angstridden in that community. A good and God fearing man, Thatcher earned a living harvesting lobsters for their shells (it would be many years before Oswald Blather discovered that lobsters were easier to eat and tasted better if you ate the meat and discarded the shells. His discovery was met with skepticism at first, resulting in his being burned at the stake. For years afterward, chastened Puritans would avoid ordering the "Surf and Turf"). Anyway, Hormel Thatcher earned enough to keep his family in penury, but one day his life changed forever when a neighbor accused him of yodeling on the Sabbath, a serious crime in those days. Professing his innocence, he stated before the congregation that it wasn't he who had yodeled, but rather it must have been a doppelganger sent by Satan. This turned out to be a mistake, as in Salem Village people were responsible for the actions of their doppelgangers, be it cursing livestock, making mischief or taping games without the expressed written consent of the Commissioner of Baseball. Hormel and his entire family were hanged, their property confiscated and their land turned into a theme park. It wasn't until 1957 that the injustice was recognized. Christian Herter, the Governor of Massachusetts, formally pardoned Thatcher, giving rise to the phrase "too little, too late".

What's in a Name?

Have you ever wondered how Smuttynose Island, located off

the coast of Portsmouth, New Hampshire, got its name? Neither have I, but the question had plagued Mehitable Sangfroid since she was a small girl growing up in nearby Newcastle. Then, on her 30th birthday in 1873, she looked it up in the local library, wondering aloud why it hadn't occurred to her to do so sooner.

Yankee Ingenuity

Octavius Winesap owned a prosperous apple orchard in Londonderry, New Hampshire. A true Yankee tinkerer, he was always looking for ways to improve his harvest and cider yield. One day, while watching some ne'er-do-wells savagely beat a tramp, an idea hit him. It was actually several of the tramp's teeth that hit him, but it inspired him nonetheless. He thought, "What if I made a device that gnashes the apples like teeth, rather than simply presses them?" Until then, the cider press was the standard way of extracting cider, but it was painstaking work. Octavius rushed home to build a prototype of his invention, but sadly he was hit by a beer wagon on the way home, so nothing ever came of it.

A Ghastly Crime

On a stiflingly hot day in August, 1892, a horrible sight greeted Dr. Tweed Markham as he visited his neighbor, Abner Brood. Brood, a notorious miser despite his success in the ready to wear bodice industry that flourished in Fairhaven, Massachusetts in the 19th century, lived in a less than elegant part of town. He shared his home with his two spinster daughters Molly and Beatrice and his trophy wife Bubbles, an exotic dancer whom he had met on a trip to Las Vegas. Dr. Tweed was surprised to find the front door ajar, as Brood was, in the words of the townfolk, "wicked paranoid". Upon entering the house and not getting an answer to his calls, he entered the sitting room. There, sprawled upon the mohair sofa was Abner Brood, his skull crushed by multiple blows from an ax.

Emotional Chaos

Alarmed, Dr. Markham ran upstairs looking for the rest of the family. He found Bubbles face down on the bedroom floor, her skull also shattered by an ax. He heard a noise from downstairs and found the younger daughter Molly washing a bloodstained ax in the kitchen sink. At the time Dr. Markham thought nothing of it, as Tuesday was traditionally ax washing day in Fairhaven, but he would later say that he should have seen it as a clue. As Molly was the only person in the house (her sister was visiting friends in New Hampshire and Bridey, the maid, was busy having a torrid affair with Lars Harmstrom, a Swedish cobbler on the other side of town), suspicion immediately fell on her. It would have been the crime of the century, but the day before a nearly identical crime occurred in Fall River involving a more prominent family named Borden. Although no one was ever convicted in either case, experts agree that this was the first "copycat" killing on record. A footnote: Twenty years later Bridey the maid went on to found General Motors.

FORGOTTEN JOBS

Our column on "Curious Tales of Old New England" prompted this letter:

"Dear Sir:

I am 88 years of age. Your column brought to mind some professions and occupations that no longer exist, or at least not to the extent that they once flourished. Of course there are some that need no explanation, such as screever, resurrectionist, answer-jobber, cragsman, grimgribber, music-duffer, nicknackitarian, jibber-jabber, phrenologist, sand-knocker, snood fitter, etc. We all know about them. I'm talking the everyday work of common folk. For example, when I was a girl, father made his living as a blimp greaser, but the Hindenburg disaster put an end to that. Therefore, I think it would be advantageous to your readers to do a column on such long lost occupations.

Sincerely,

Thelia Baxter Knolton

PS How about those Red Sox?"

Since we couldn't think of anything else to write about, we did some research and found out about some other jobs that have gone the way of the Milkman, Scissor Grinder, Diaper Service Man, Rug Braider, Hobo Skinner, Calling Card Refurbisher, Barn Owl Sexer, Door to Door Gutter Snipe and Hat Blocker:

Knob Polisher

In the tradition of the Scissor Grinder, the Knob Polisher would go from town to town with his colorfully painted wagon calling out "Bring out your knobs! Door knobs, drawer knobs, four

Emotional Chaos

knobs, more knobs! Bring out your knobs!" Housewives (or their maids, if they were among the well to do) would bring out their knobs to be polished, refurbished or even replaced. Some would go into people's houses and polish their knobs, but that was a more specialized field.

Lint Collector

(as opposed to the Dust Gatherer, who really didn't do much of anything). The Lint Collector would go door to door asking for lint. On a good laundry day he could collect up to two pounds of it. What he did with it was anyone's guess.

Servant Flogger

The most famous of these was Ossip Bulow of Hartford, Connecticut. A German immigrant who made his fortune providing powdered bratwurst to the Union Army during the Civil War, Bulow never charged for his services. He saw servant flogging as "A way of giving back to the country that gave me so much".

Pincushion Stuffer

In the days when every woman learned to sew at a young age, the pincushion industry boomed. It was a way for young immigrant women to start a home business of their own, or even work their way into the more lucrative sweatshop trade.

Medicine Bottle Label Gluer

This was popular for orphans who couldn't get a coveted street urchin position. There were several popular patent medicines at the time such as Carter's Little Liver Pills; McCoy's Miraculous Nerve Tonic; Dr. Frobisher's Night Terror Suppressant; Scanlon's Scurvy Scourge, Nurse Missy's Colic Cure and Moose Laxative; Mother Kindness's Mercury Drops, Carstairs Brothers Laudanum

Emotional Chaos

Pops, etc. In the days before the assembly line, label gluing was painstaking, demanding work. Plus, as label glue was extremely toxic, the turnover rate was high.

Ham Loft Supervisor

In the time before refrigeration most people canned, dried, pickled or otherwise preserved food for the long winter. Hams were especially popular, although not many people had room to store them. Every town of any size had a ham loft, and looking after the hams was the duty of a highly specialized individual. After serving a long apprenticeship as a ham curer, an especially industrious or clever individual could demonstrate the skills necessary for this exacting task. Often, it was passed from generation to generation. (Editor's note: Some historians believe that this is why Jewish immigrants faced discrimination when they arrived in America. Some, eager to assimilate, turned their back on keeping kosher and "Took Up The Ham").

Dog Shooter

In the days before Humane Societies, putting down an old family pet or rabid animal fell to whoever was closest to the shotgun. For people without firearms, however, it was necessary to call the Dog Shooter, Cat Drowner, Rabbit Stomper or Goat Intimidator.

Pinecone Man

Usually a colorful eccentric, the Pinecone Man would roam the woods looking for pinecones. Pinecones were once a thriving industry, especially in New Hampshire (see also "Pine Needle Sweeper"), but once synthetic pinecones were introduced in the 1940s, the Pinecone Man all but disappeared.

SIGNS, SIGNS, EVERYWHERE ARE SIGNS

The ability to read signs, omens, entrails, tea leaves, etc. has been with us for millennia. People with "The Gift" called "sages", "oracles", "witches" and "weirdos" have been feared, respected and invited to all the best parties. If you could tell the future you had it made, right?

Maybe not. True, sages and seers from time immemorial have been predicting the future, channeling for the gods and giving advice, so there must be something to it, you say. Yes, it's true that this often resulted in a pretty good paycheck, but on the flip side it often resulted in a burning at the stake. The trick was to keep it vague, rather like a modern horoscope. Do you ever pick up the paper and read "You will be hit by the Number 10 bus today; you might want to stock up on aspirin"? Of course not. Keep it simple, like:

"Fortune smiles on those who dare", or "someone from your past will breathe oxygen today". Your smarter sages have known this for years. Witness this classic exchange between King Philco of the Thracian city-state of Harmonica and the great sage Persimmon:

King Philco: "What news of Troy? Is this the day to launch my forces and smite my enemies?"

Persimmon: "When the golden turtle swims the Tigris River and the thrush sings at midnight, Agamemnon will feel the sting of a rash!"

Queen Amana: "See? I told you! The minute I saw his ad at the Acropolis, the one that said 'It's like having the Oracle at Delphi in your living room!', I knew he was the right sage for us!"

Personally, I think the gods must have better things to do than spend their times sending obtuse signs to mortals. I mean, if you're omnipotent, can't you think of a better way to communicate your wishes to the lowly than singing thrushes or golden turtles? A Candygram would be better, even if it came COD.

The Greek gods were masters of this. They played mortal man like a Stradivarius (which hadn't been invented yet, but it makes for a good example). They screwed around with the mortals' heads so much that the Greeks wrote works like The Iliad and The Odyssey as a record for future lawsuits. Luckily for the gods, lawyers hadn't been invented yet either, which was the major reason it was called The Golden Age of Civilization.

Now the God of the Old Testament had the right idea. When God wanted man's attention, you can be sure He didn't beat around the bush. In fact, a burning bush was about as subtle as He got. Usually it was plagues of Biblical proportions, edicts to off the first born, angels with flaming swords, etc. No namby-pamby singing thrushes for Him. Smiting the wicked usually got the message across, and if man was too dense to figure out God's plan a plague of locusts usually did the trick. Or a flaming lawyer.

Nowadays, of course, people are too sophisticated to believe in omens. Luck, The Psychic Network and Alan Greenspan, maybe, but not omens.

A good example of this is Wildfire, one of those sappy songs from the 1970s about a guy whose lover used to ride around Nebraska on a horse named, you guessed it, "Wildfire". Then, one night tragedy struck. The titular beast got spooked by a blizzard, or the early onset of frost (the lyrics are a little vague as to the actual cause of death), busted out of its stall, ran out into the night and snuffed it. Not being clever, she ran out after it and also died. You'd think someone living in the Midwest would know better. Anyway, that should have been the end of it beyond a trip to the Alpo factory, but no. The hero of the song starts seeing obtuse signs involving hoot'owls making a racket outside his window for close to a week. What I want to know is, how does the singer draw a connection between noisy birds and the return of his dead lover and her equally dead horse? And why are they back? Is

Emotional Chaos

Wildfire upset that he was stabled in such a cheap stall that he could easily kick it down and head out into the storm? Maybe it's paranoia. Or guilt. Was the horse heavily insured? And where does natural selection fit into all this? Maybe I'm being too harsh; I hear Mr. Ed went the same way.

So, is the singer seeing signs or just being paranoid? It's hard to say. I don't know about you, but if some spectral being was coming for me in the night, I'd be paranoid, too.

But, as Freud once said, sometimes a hoot'owl is just a hoot'owl.

IS LIFE A BEACH?

Every year about this time, various publications with nothing better to do run the obligatory "My favorite beach" article. They fill their Lifestyle sections with pieces written by staffers about where they like to go to loll in the sand, play in the waves, develop early skin cancer, etc.

Smaller magazines will focus on local beaches, of which there's no shortage here in New England, at least along the coast. There are relatively few beaches in Aroostook county, at least not of the sort where the Beautiful People congregate. In the high end travel magazines (you know the kind; slick, glossy publications with ads for exclusive resorts, Jaguars and $15,000 watches), the writers extol the virtues of places like The Singing Sands of St. Vitus or the black sand beaches of the Yellow Sea (or is it the yellow sand beaches of the Black Sea?). These are exotic places that regular Joes like you and I will never see. In fact, I think they don't even exist. But then, I felt the same way about New Jersey until it was proven otherwise.

It's time that those of us wise enough to avoid the beach had a say in the matter or, to paraphrase General Philip Sheridan, "The only good beach is an empty beach". For folks like us, spending a day at the beach is about as pleasurable as a root canal with a rusty ice pick.

Why, you ask? It seems pretty obvious to those of us in the know, but I'll explain it anyway, as I'm only halfway through the column. Here are just some of the reasons that I avoid the beach:

The heat. Beachgoers claim that they go to the beach to get away from the heat. This is like saying you go to Walmart to avoid people wearing polyester. A beach is an unsheltered, highly reflective place that magnifies the heat. What about the sea breeze, you say? What about air conditioning, I say. It's a lot more consistent and can be enjoyed in the comfort of your own home.

Emotional Chaos

Sand. Sand is gritty, uncomfortable and gets into all kinds of places it doesn't belong. I suppose there are those who enjoy wearing a sandpaper jockstrap, but that's between them and their therapists.

Suntan lotion. Why go someplace where you have to slather yourself with grease? Plus, the aforementioned sand sticks to the grease, making the situation even more uncomfortable. For me, the sickening smell of suntan lotion has the same Proustian flashback quality that cordite had to a shell-shocked Doughboy.

Swimming in the ocean. I like to swim in pools, even lakes. The ocean is different. Now, I've never been to the Bahamas, or Aruba or anyplace else where the water is crystal clear. Here in the Northeast the water is ominously dark, full of unseen slimy things and sharp objects. And there's the cold. Even on days when it's like Saudi Arabia in the off season, the water here is so cold that by the time you're in up to your calves you can't feel your feet. Which is probably just as well, as that way you can't see what you're about to step on. For those who say, "the cold water is bracing on a hot day!" I have one word: undertow.

The wildlife. In addition to what's lurking beneath the waves, the beach is a gathering spot for all sorts of unpleasant fauna. First on the list is seagulls. I've seen seagulls so nasty that they attack and eat pigeons, which isn't necessarily a bad thing. The ones around here begging (or, more appropriately demanding at gunpoint) fries, clams, cash, etc. are particularly aggressive. Then there's the small, biting insects. No beach is free of them, it's only the degree of annoyance.

I could go on all day, but I'm out of space. Still, if these folks want to congregate at the beach, let them. I'll be inside in the air conditioned shade.

THE CHICKEN OF
THE BLUNDERVILLES:
AN INSPECTOR BLANCMANGE MYSTERY

Part 1: Murder Most Fowl

It was one of those days unique to London; a cold, dank day when ennui filled the air and the fog was so thick it seemed one could jump out the window and be wafted to the ground as if on a feather pillow.

"Remember when I jumped out the window expecting to be wafted to the ground as if on a feather pillow, Blancmange?" said Colonel Broadbeam, late of the Royal Horse Marines and biographer of Inspector Blancmange.

"Yes, my dear fellow. As I recall you were in traction for six months. I must write a monograph on that episode!"

Just then, there came a knock on the door.

"I think you'll find, Broadbeam, that there's someone knocking at the door."

"How do you do it, Blancmange?" Broadbeam asked, with understandable admiration.

"Well, for one thing, I'm not brain damaged from jumping out of windows" Blancmange thought, but chose not to express aloud. "I suspect that for someone to venture out in this beastly weather they must be sorely in need of our services!"

Once again the Great Detective was correct. When Broadbeam answered the door, standing in the hallway was none other than young Sir Charles Blunderville, son of the late Lord Bevis Blunderville.

"Come in, Sir Charles, and warm yourself by the fire!" said Blancmange, "I trust you're here to seek my help in solving the brutal murder of your father!"

Emotional Chaos

"You must be able to read minds, Inspector!" said Blunderville. "Or is it because of the unusual circumstances of his death that have been so recently sensationalized in the tabloids?"

"You must admit, my dear Sir Charles, it's not every day that a man meets his end in such a way. It took quite a sensational demise to move Jack the Ripper off the front page of the Times!"

"I would not have believed it myself, had I not seen the results with my own eyes. You see, Blunderville Hall, our ancestral home, is situated in the Macken Mire, a bleak and godforsaken place on the Brackish Moors. When one spends his life in a place such as that, one sees many strange things. Things beyond the ken of mortal man, indeed, things no doubt beyond the ken of a merciful Heaven! But this episode was bizarre even by the standards of that profane and wicked place!"

"I say!" said Broadbeam.

"Yes, so I can say it would appear to be true, gentlemen, just as was reported in the popular press! My father was pecked to death by a huge, demonic chicken!"

"I say!" said Broadbeam.

Blancmange lit his pipe. "Surely a man of science such as yourself doesn't believe in such things! I've read your works on tuba playing among the Hottentot, and your paper on dementia in kelp is something of a classic! So, then, Sir Charles, why do you seek our services? Surely not to trap this hellish fowl."

"No, Inspector. Unlike the simple folk who live on the moors, I have no superstitious belief in ghosts, wraiths, banshees, demonic chickens or the glowing hedgehog that's said to make its appearance every Guy Fawkes Day. No, I know my father was murdered, and it was not by any supernatural livestock! The chicken was merely the instrument of his demise, manipulated by some Svengali for reasons unknown. But, there's more, Inspector Blancmange! Since his death at the hands, er, beak of the chicken, strange things have been happening at Blunderville Hall!"

"I say!" said Broadbeam.

"Broadbeam," said Blancmange patiently, "Doesn't the fog look soft and inviting?"

"So it does, Blancmange! I'll wager that one could jump out the window and be wafted to the ground as if on a feather pillow!" He proceeded to put his theory to the test, with predictable results.

"Well, Sir Charles, now that that's out of the way, tell me about these curious events."

"As I was saying, strange things have occurred beyond my father's death. First, Puckish, my manservant, was found in the oven, trussed up and stuffed with bread crumbs! That very night, my favorite boots, which I'd left out on the sidewalk to be blacked, disappeared! Then, as a final straw, someone replaced my regular coffee with Folger's Crystals!"

"This is curious, indeed! I think a trip to Blunderville Hall is called for! We shall leave on the noon train from Paddington Station. We must get to the bottom of this before this poultry manipulating fiend strikes again!"

"You can't imagine how grateful I am, Inspector!"

"I say!" said Broadbeam, entering the room disheveled but none the worse for his adventure. "Luckily, a street urchin broke my fall. Oh, well, plenty more where HE came from, eh?"

And with that they all had a good laugh.

Part 2: Don't Count Your Chickens Before They Kill

The next day dawned clear and full of promise. The noon train from Paddington Station took Blancmange, Broadbeam and Sir Charles to Bleekmoor, where they took a connecting train to Dintymoor. From there they took a carriage to the village of Pusworth, on the edge of the Brackish Moors. They lunched at the Knacker's Yard tavern before proceeding to Blunderville Hall, situated in the Macken Mire, deep in the heart of the Moor.

Emotional Chaos

"Did you notice they way the locals were looking at us at the tavern, Blancmange?" Colonel Broadbeam said in the carriage as they rode through the bleak and twisted landscape. Sir Charles hadn't exaggerated, it was a beastly place. "The way the innkeeper's wife warned us to stay off the Moor before she read the specials? The fact that there was no chicken to be found on the menu? No chicken at all?!"

"Yes, my dear Broadbeam. Country folk are a superstitious lot. We must seem strange to them, going out on the Moor and into the Macken Mire by choice. Plus the fact that you used your waistcoat as a napkin."

"It's a habit I picked up in India."

"Yes, you picked up various social diseases, too, but that's no reason to continue the practice. But that's beside the point. Sir Charles, who lives in that stone cottage? It seems the only structure on the Moor."

"I don't think it's been used since the bronze age. As you may have noticed, real estate doesn't exactly move around these parts."

"Curious", said Blancmange. He then fell into a silence for the rest of the journey, as he often did when deeply under the influence of marijuana. After an hour's time the carriage approached the forbidding edifice of Blunderville Hall.

"Welcome to my family's home gentlemen!" said Sir Charles. Two wretched creatures stood in the driveway. "There's Dawks, the butler, and Frothingmouth, the gamekeeper. Other than that, the only servants are Mrs. Dawks, my cook and housekeeper, and Bridget, the stereotypical Irish maid."

"I don't think we'll find our killer among your household staff, Sir Charles. This was clearly a crime of cunning and intellect."

"I hope you're right, Inspector! I'd hate to think that such a fiend is under my own roof!"

Blancmange made no comment about what was under his roof. Dawks took their baggage into the house while Frothingmouth led the horses away. He looked no stranger to violence, but looks can be deceiving. Blancmange had learned that hard lesson early in his career. In that instance, so many years before, he had been so taken by the charms of one Miss Penelope Bane that he never suspected that delicate beauty of being the Manchester Mangler. Forced to drown her in a bucket of cider, he would bear the physical and emotional scars the rest of his days. Blancmange would rarely speak of her, but when he did he always called her simply "That Woman" or "That Woman with the Large Ice Axe".

That evening at dinner, Blancmange asked Mrs. Dawks about the legendary demonic chicken, as she was born in Pusworth and had spent her entire life in the shadow of the Brackish Moors.

"Aye sir, folks round these parts could tell you stories! I never seen the demon bird myself, but I know plenty who 'ave and lived to tell the tale! And plenty who 'aven't!"

"Haven't what?" asked Broadbeam, daubing the gravy from his mouth with his waistcoat.

"Haven't lived to tell the tale, sir!" God, she thought, these big city types are thick.

"And don't forget that glowing hedgehog! Every Guy Fawkes Day it comes, faith and begorra!" Bridget chimed in.

"Surely you don't believe such nonsense!" Broadbeam said, "Demonic chickens! Glowing hedgehogs! Rubbish!"

"Mock as you may sir, but many an unlucky soul has wandered onto the Moors only to be found, pecked to death in a most 'orrible fashion!"

Blancmange interrupted, "Right now, we're interested in the murder of Sir Bevis Blunderville. By the way, Mrs. Dawks, this haggis is excellent! You must give the recipe to my housekeeper, Mrs. Desoto!"

Mrs. Dawks beamed. "Kind of you to say, sir! The secret is the proper sheep's stomach!"

"Do you have any recipes for... chicken?"

The lightning flashed significantly, even though it had been clear a moment before.

"Why... no, sir.... well, folks round these parts..."

"Thank you, Mrs. Dawks! Gentlemen, I suggest we retire to the billiard room!"

Once Blancmange, Broadbeam and Sir Charles had retired to the billiard room, Sir Charles asked, "What was that about, Blancmange?"

"These provincials are so frightened by their superstitions that they can't bear even the thought of poultry!"

"But what could it mean, Blancmange?"

"Everything and nothing, Sir Charles! Everything and nothing"!

Part 3: A Peck of Trouble

Once removed to the privacy of the billiard room, Blancmange was free to explain to Broadbeam and Sir Charles.

"You'll forgive my evasiveness gentlemen, but in a place such as this the walls have ears!"

"They came with the house", said Sir Charles defensively, "Beastly things, really, but my father insisted on leaving them up there as a warning to the servants."

"Speaking of the servants, would you be so kind as to summon yours to the library? I have an announcement to make that will be of interest to all in the household!"

Blancmange, Broadbeam and Sir Charles went to the library, where Sir Charles rang the bell to summon Dawks, Mrs. Dawks, Frothingmouth and Bridget. When they were assembled, Blanc-mange spoke.

"I suppose you're wondering why I should summon you all."

"Is it Guy Fawkes Day? Is the glowing hedgehog about?" asked

Bridget brightly.

"If I may continue", said Blancmange, pouring a glass of port and lighting up a large joint, "The reason for this gathering is to announce that Dawks, the butler, is really Captain Eustis Plunk-Cavendish!"

"I say!" said Broadbeam, "Surely not THE Captain Eustis Plunk-Cavendish, Blancmange!"

"The same! And Mrs. Dawks is in fact his wife, Ammonia Plunk-Cavendish"

"I say!" said Broadbeam.

"And Bridget, the stereotypical Irish maid, is none other than Prudence, the illegitimate daughter born of his now notorious relationship with Judith Flemm, a scullery maid at Sandhurst!" He put the joint to his lips and drew the smoke deeply into his lungs.

"The layers of deception run deep, gentlemen, very deep indeed!"

"What about Frothingmouth, the gamekeeper?"

"He's just the gamekeeper."

Sir Charles said, "Who is this Captain Eustis Plunk-Cavendish? As you know, I was looking after my holdings in Canada for some seven years before my father's brutal demise brought me back to Blunderville Hall, so I've not heard any news beyond the hockey scores."

"Forgive me, my dear Sir Charles! I forget sometimes how slowly the news travels to the provinces! Captain Eustis Plunk-Cavendish committed the murder of one of our nations greatest heroes, Field Marshal Augustus Tiberius Spottswode!"

"Field Marshal Spottswode? The Hero of the Punjab Uprising and Exterminator of the Zulus?"

"The very same! Despite the fact that Plunk-Cavendish has been surgically altered to resemble Benjamin Disraeli, I immediately recognized the fiend! The eyes don't lie, gentlemen! I can always tell the wicked by the glint of evil in their eyes! I couldn't let on, of course, otherwise he'd disappear into the Macken Mire, perhaps never to be seen again!"

"But why did he kill such a beloved hero as Field Marshal Spottswode?" asked Sir Charles.

"Perhaps Captain Plunk-Cavendish would like to answer that."

Plunk-Cavendish only glared at Blancmange, his Disraeli-like face a mask of hatred and rage.

"No? Then I'll tell the story. You see, many years ago Plunk-Cavendish was an aide to Field Marshall Spottswode, and a promising young officer at that. But something happened. An invasion plan. A plan, seemingly feasible but doomed to fail!"

"It was a sound plan!!" Plunk-Cavendish roared, lunging forward. Blancmange, a master of Jeet-Jaju, deftly stepped aside and hit him with a large ashtray.

"Your plans to invade the Dalmatian Coast were spotty at best! Field Marshal Spottswode knew that, and that's why you killed him!"

"Blast your eyes, Blancmange! I should have killed you when I had the chance!"

Blancmange was nonplussed. "I took the liberty of having Inspector Glucose and Sergeant Haffwitt secrete themselves in the stone cottage on the moor. They should arrive momentarily! There's no escape from justice this time, my dear Plunk-Cavendish!"

Just then Inspector Glucose and Sergeant Haffwitt entered through the window.

"You could have used the door, gentlemen!" said Sir Charles.

"There will be time for that later, Sir Charles!", said Blancmange, "I dare say that Plunk-Cavendish, Mrs. Plunk-Cavendish and Prudence all have a date with the hangman!"

"Beg pardon, sir", said Sergeant Haffwitt, "But maybe we

should hang Frothingmouth too, just to be on the safe side!"

"Good thinking, Sergeant", said Glucose, "You'll make Inspector some day! Round them up and take them away!"

"Well!" said Blancmange, "That clears up that mystery!"

"I say!" said Broadbeam, "This is all well and good, but what about the demonic chicken? What about Lord Bevis' violent death?"

"One case at a time, my dear Broadbeam, one case at a time!"

And with that they all had a good laugh.

MORE CURIOUS TALES OF
OLD NEW ENGLAND

It's Witchcraft!

After the Salem witch hysteria of the 1690s, a lot of other towns learned a valuable lesson in religious tolerance and the true meaning of justice. The nearby hamlet of Unstable, Massachusetts, (pronounced UN-stable) however, saw it as an opportunity. Not being as prosperous or well situated as Salem Village, the people of Unstable were always scrambling for ways to make money and attract new settlers. Cheap land, free kine with every plot of land purchased (which would have been more successful if they said "livestock"), nothing worked. Maybe because Unstable was situated on both a swamp and an Indian burial ground made it undesirable, no one knew. Then one day, the Reverend Decrease Witherspoon was reading the stories of the goings on in Salem and had an idea: what if Unstable had its own witch trials? They could turn a travesty into a tourist attraction! First, of course, they needed witches. That was the easy part, being accused of witchcraft in Colonial New England was as easy as falling off a log. In fact, one could be proven a witch by the inability to stay on a log. The obvious choice as the first to be accused was Whippet Goode, a curious and eccentric young woman. Still unmarried at the age of 14, and still possessing all her teeth at the age of 25, she had always attracted the suspicion and envy of her neighbors. The fact that she made her living as a door to door broom and black cat peddler sealed the deal. During a well publicized trial, she was asked to name names. She eventually named Thaddeus Stark, a greengrocer, Anesthesia Hutchinson, a housewife, Lassie Bidwell, a midwife, Charity Hasp, a housemaid and Clapper Hoarfrost, a ne'er-do-well. She also named all of the judges who were in the court at the time, but that testimony ended up on the cutting room floor. The accused were hanged in the public square. Despite the great injustice, the tactic worked and soon Unstable was a thriving town. To this day they say the ghost of Whippet Goode haunts the town, usually showing up at the local Dairy Queen.

The Man Who Made Turnips a Household Name

Everyone knows about Johnny Appleseed, born John Chapman, near Leominster, Massachusetts. Little is known of the man called "Josie Turnipseed", except that he was born Josiah Turner in Chelsea, Massachusetts in 1821. Seeing the good work that Johnny Appleseed did in his travels across America, he changed his name to Josie Turnipseed and embarked on a journey to bring turnips to the nation. Even though no one actually likes turnips, he was successful enough to spawn a host of imitators, including Peter Pumpkinseed, Cedric Celerystalk, Virgil Vidaliaonion and Arthur Artichokeheart, as well as Mortimer Manure, Comstock Compost and Waldo Weedbegone. Soon there were so many barefoot eccentrics migrating west that the shortage became noticeable in New England, leading to laws being passed.

Forgotten Delicacies

All New Englanders have enjoyed such regional favorites as brown bread, boiled dinner, fried clams, Indian pudding, blueberry muffins, etc. But a recently unearthed cookbook (Literally. It was found buried under the midden heap of what was once the farm of Constant Hornblower in Upwind, New Hampshire during a recent archeological dig) showed that early settlers enjoyed such delicacies as: roast cauliflower in huckleberry sauce, quahog pudding with nutmeg syrup, pinecone gravy, grape duff, suet candy and fishbone fritters. Culinary scholars have concluded that it comes as no surprise that the book was buried under a midden heap where it belonged.

Emotional Chaos

The Mayor Who Banned Leaf Peeping

Even though people have enjoyed the spectacular New England foliage since the days the Indians roamed the land, not many people realize that it was once illegal to do so in Stockbroth, Vermont. In 1924, Hamish Pillock Newelpost, mayor of Stockbroth, passed a law "prohibiting travel for the purpose of gawking at trees just because it's fall". Because foliage tours were very popular and added much to the town coffers, the citizens were baffled. "What's the big deal with trees?" Newelpost would ask if pressed on the issue, "You see one you've seen 'em all". When it was discovered that he was color-blind he was run out of town on a rail.

The Fish Whisperer

New Englanders have long made their living from the bounty of the sea. Hutchinson Wheelwright, of Unctuous Cove, Maine was known far and wide as "The Fish Whisperer". It was said he could stick his head underwater and convince fish to surrender willingly to the nets of the local fisherman. He died tragically when, in a deep philosophical conversation with a haddock, he stayed underwater too long and drowned.

LEGENDS OF THE OLD WEST AND HOW THEY GREW

The Old West was full of larger than life characters: Buffalo Bill Cody, Butch Cassidy and the Sundance Kid, Annie Oakley, Wild Bill Hickok, Belle Starr, Jesse James, Billy the Kid. Everyone knows the story of the OK Corral, how the Earps and Doc Holliday faced off against the Clantons and some other guys, how Pat Garrett shot Billy The Kid, how Cool Hand Luke ate fifty eggs... oh, wait, that was a movie. But Paul Newman and George Kennedy were in it, and they made a lot of westerns. And let's not forget about Strother Martin. Anyway, the lore of the West has fascinated us for a hundred years and spawned a hundred tales (give or take. The lawyers made us put that in).

One of the most notorious gunmen of the Old West was "Angry Bill" Boskovitch. Boskovitch gave his favorite pastime as "shootin' folks". It must have been a hobby he enjoyed immensely, as by the time of his death he had killed 4,274 men, women and children (he liked killing animals, too, but no one kept an accurate count). One reason for this astonishingly high body count is that towards the end of his life, as his reputation grew, it became a great honor to be shot by Angry Bill. Wherever he went, people would come from miles around to provoke him to violence. "Nyah, nyah, huckleberry, can't hit the side of a barn!", they would taunt. While this almost always resulted in a fatal shooting, it did insure a sort of immortality and gave one's family something to brag about.

Perhaps the most vicious killer in the West was Wilfred Skagg. Skagg showed a mean streak from an early age. Angered by being named "Wilfred", he shot his parents at age 4 and went on a killing spree that even Billy the Kid called "an inspiration". Having read that John Wesley Hardin once shot a man just for snoring, Skagg outdid him by shooting a man just for adhering to Hegel's philosophy of Phenomenology of Mind. "The ultimate truth of the universal is self-conscious of itself as absolute spirit, my eye!", he sneered, standing over the man's twitching corpse. Not content with killing those who differed with him philosophically, Skagg killed people for all sorts of reasons: wearing spurs that jingle jangle jingle, eating hominy out of season, having been born in Wisconsin and using the word "varmint" in a Scrabble game. He met his demise as he had lived, violently. He was playing poker in a saloon when a crazed Lithuanian, mistaking him for Archduke Franz Josef Habsburgh, stabbed him repeatedly with a salad fork. The hand he was holding, five deuces, became known as "a bunch of cards with blood all over them".

Wyatt Earp and Wild Bill Hickok weren't the only famous lawmen who sometimes trod both sides of justice. A famous gunslinger turned lawman turned gunslinger turned lawman turned nun turned gunslinger was Alonzo Pepper. Pepper, besides having serious identity issues, knew that the best way to enforce the law was to think like an outlaw. He did this so well that he frequently robbed banks "just for research", although he always kept the money. During his last period of lawlessness he teamed up with the notorious Blanche Terwilliger, aka "Dance Hall Minnie". The two of them cut a swath across New Mexico until they realized they'd left the gas on and went back. Returning to their swath, they were ambushed by "Waco Jack" Dullard, the sheriff of Taos. His deed was immortalized in the "Ballad of Dullard", although the ballad took several liberties with the facts (for example, Dullard claims he shot Alonzo and Minnie while they were robbing the Tucson stage. Actually, they were sleeping).

Blanche Terwilliger wasn't as famous as Belle Starr or Calamity Jane, but she was much more famous than Saluda Montez, aka "Mexican Kate". No one knew why Mexican Kate was notorious; historians think it was an effective PR campaign. A more well documented Lady of the West was Etta Winchester, aka "Morey Amsterdam". Etta began her career as a dance hall girl, worked her way up to madam but, hitting the prostitution glass ceiling,

Emotional Chaos

turned to a life of crime. She was hanged in Tombstone on August 8, 1899, the last woman hanged there until the following Thursday.

Many a tome has been written about the Old West. Why does it fascinate us so, even to this day? Is it a longing for a bygone era when a man lived by his wits and his word? The freedom, the pioneer spirit, the total lack of personal hygiene and respect for human life? Hegel said it best: "These people are crazy!"

Emotional Chaos

WATCH THE SKIES

Those of us who remember Project Blue Book, the Air Force's investigation into UFO sightings back in the 1960s, are surely wondering whatever happened to all those UFOs. In those days, the skies were lousy with UFOs, strange lights and all sorts of weird and unexplainable things. So why have sightings dropped off? Have the aliens lost interest? Or is it us? We have more cable channels now than we ever dreamed of back then, so staring up at the night sky has lost a lot of the appeal it had back in the days when we were limited to network TV. Coincidence? Maybe not.

How did it all start, you ask? It began in a small town named Roswell, New Mexico (and we're being generous here. "God forsaken wasteland" might have been a more apt description. Now, before you Roswellians start sending angry letters and e-mails threatening lawsuits and rectal probes, let me say that I'm sure Roswell is a nice place. What I'm saying is that in 1947 it wasn't exactly Paris in springtime).

People around Roswell began seeing what were described as "Flying Saucers". Before that, UFOs had been known as "Warp Drive Interstellar Spacecraft", but "Flying Saucers" looked better in the tabloids. Reliable (by the standards of the day, given the amount of alcohol consumption back then) sources even reported seeing wreckage and bodies of aliens described as "really mangled, but hey, you try to look good after a UFO crash". It seemed like a slam-dunk: our neighbors from beyond the solar system were visiting, and boy, were they lousy drivers. But then, something happened. With all the attention being focused on this small hamlet, as well as increasing paranoia over the Cold War (when, apparently, there was a Communist under the bed, if only for emergencies), the Government backpedaled on the claims that aliens had indeed landed/crashed/stopped for a quick bite in Roswell. Soon very convincing pictures of military officers holding wreckage were described as "downed weather balloons" rather then "the debris from the crash of a highly sophisticated interstellar vehicle". In fact, they were quite insistent about it when dealing with the locals. "Listen, rube", they'd say with more than a little menace, "That glowing, spinning thing you saw do an Immelmann roll over your dirt farm and then shoot up at Mach 6 and crash with a blast roughly the size of Hiroshima was just a weather balloon". Some, like Cletus Flemm remained skeptical:

Cletus: "Wouldn't it be more convincing to tell me it was a top secret experimental aircraft from the nearby Air Force base, which, as I recall, spends most of its time testing top secret experimental aircraft?"

Major: "Uh, I suppose..."

Captain: "Hey, that WOULD make more sense!"

Cletus: "I mean, THAT I'd believe, or even, 'It's a matter of national security, so don't tell anyone'. But a weather balloon? How dumb, drunk and inbred do you think I am?"

Major: "Well, you DO live in a packing crate."

Captain: "And your wife does bear a striking resemblance to you. Close enough to be your sister!"

Cletus: "Twin. But that's besides the point. Before you came, I'd have believed anything the government told me, but now I'm afraid I'll have to tell the tabloids."

Cletus never did, of course, as he was never seen again, but somehow the word got out. Soon, everyone was watching the skies for UFOs.

And what of the aliens themselves? Beings that have mastered deep space travel seem to have certain glaring limitations. For openers, they always dress alike, usually in jumpsuits (they seem to favor silver or sparkly synthetic materials. I always suspected a connection between aliens and disco). And why do such advanced beings rely so much on rectal probes to gather information? Do they know something we don't? What happened to the Star Trek scanners, the ones that Bones would simply wave around and obtain such key information as, "Jim, this man's a Klingon!". He never had to say, "Bend over" to learn what he needed to know. In fact, you never heard him say, "Turn your head and cough", either. That's MY idea of advanced medicine!

So, is there a method to their madness? Are they trying to keep us guessing? The aliens always try to maintain a low profile (or as low as one can in a glowing, spinning spacecraft that looks like a Christmas tree in heat). They never land anyplace where the collective IQ is beyond the double digits, either. Maybe that's why they have such a low opinion of us. It can't simply be from monitoring our television broadcasts. If they based their opinion of us on that they would have vaporized the planet by now.

In the early 1960s there was another spate of sightings a continent away, in the middle of the Pacific Ocean. But, as no one lives there, we turn to a spate of sightings a continent away in the other direction. Suddenly there was a rash of UFO sightings in New Hampshire, especially in the White Mountain regions. Why? Given the population of New Hampshire at the time, it fits the pattern of chosen contactees. Now that southern New Hampshire is overrun with economic refugees fleeing Massachusetts, the UFO sightings have dropped off precipitously. More than coincidence? We think not. But that's a story for another day.

A pattern has emerged, but the question is why? Is there a method to their madness? Are they trying to keep us guessing? Unless they choose to make a bold statement like blowing up the White House (as in Independence Day), or landing in Times Square (although who'd know, if you've been to Times Square lately), the aliens always try to maintain a low profile that borders on the anti-social. Why are the folks who have "Close Encounters" with "UFOs", usually after a "Night of Drinking" and "Wild Sex with Lurleen" in the "Bed of the Pickup" a prime target for such encounters? Let's look a the most common "contactee" and "abductee" profile. They generally:

Emotional Chaos

Live in the middle of nowhere.

Live in a trailer or shotgun shack (never a ranch in the suburbs, a condo or even a McMansion, although most of us would like to see those get the Independence Day treatment).

Rarely possess a full complement of teeth.

Don't mind discussing their rectal probes on daytime TV talk shows.

We decided to seek out some of these people to find out their take on the situation. One such person is Corneilia-Jo Mange of Dungheap, Nevada, who lives in a double wide in the desert and makes crafts out of tin cans and old rattlesnakes. Cornelia-Jo writes, "UFOs land here all the time. It's getting so I'm going to have to start charging for the probings. That's why I moved to Nevada. You can do that here."

Another famous case involved Billy Bob Crisco, a highway scraper in Lemmingston, New Hampshire, who claims to have been abducted in 1964. He agreed to tell his story for a case of Budweiser and a used Playboy.

"I was comin' home from a NASCAR support group, drivin' down Route 93, where I do most of my best animal scrapin', when I seen this real bright glowing light up ahead. I figured it was one of them UFOs I was hearin' so much about, so I went to see what was goin' on. The next thing I remember I woke up in an artist's loft in Paris with no recollection of the past three years. I guess I had a one man show in Montmartre, but it met with poor critical reviews so I came home".

Under hypnosis, however, a very different tale emerged. Billy Bob left his pickup to investigate the mysterious object. It was a glowing, spherical craft manned by beings he called "strangely carnival like", with small bodies, large heads, dark, blank eyes and matching silver jumpsuits. They told him telepathically not to be afraid and them probed him until dawn. He woke up in his truck and went to work. The whole Paris thing turned out to be an implanted memory, although the critics could have been kinder.

So now we have to ask ourselves two important questions: One, will the aliens someday openly make contact with us? Two, is there an active government cover-up of the whole thing? And why? I'd answer that, but I said there would be two questions.

One thing is certain. The authorities acted quickly to deny the early reports of crashed "flying saucers", alien corpses and missing witnesses. In fact, many newspapers carried an AP story that said: "Reports of flying saucers whizzing through the sky fell off sharply today as the government began a concentrated campaign to stop the rumors."

It was quite effective. Just ask Cletus.

LIGHTS, CAMERA, DEATH:
A SPIKE SLAMMER MYSTERY

There's one thing about working in Tinseltown: It's a freak show, but some of the freaks have the moolah to hire a private dick like me. Separating the rich and famous from their dough is a time honored tradition in Hollywood, be it blackmail, marriage, scams, crazy investments or just plain gouging. The more they pay the better they feel, like junkies with a platinum card instead of a needle. A dame I know over at MGM said a starlet there paid $50,000 for a dress. For that they ought to throw in shoes, a belt and a broad to wear it who's willing to earn her money the hard way.

And speaking of earning money, I was on my way to meet with an actor who was having the screws put to him by a loan shark. Apparently this mook was into the shylocks for some serious green, and they were threatening to reposition his moneymaker if he didn't pay up. About six blocks from his body, to be exact. I'd seen this guy's work, and from what I could tell he chewed the scenery like a starving Ethiopian in a gingerbread house. Still, as long as the check cleared I wasn't particular.

I turned my Desoto into the lot at Paregoric Pictures and told the guard I was looking for Tom Tellmark. He wasn't impressed. I guess he'd seen all the stars. He was seeing stars when I left him, all right, but not the film kind. I went to Tellmark's bungalow and rang the bell.

"Who's there?" a frightened voice called from inside.

"Slammer. Spike Slammer. The shamus you hired."

The door opened a crack and I saw one bloodshot eye dart around. He undid more chains than a dominatrix and opened the door. He looked shorter than he did on screen.

Emotional Chaos

"I'm sorry if I seem nervous, Mr. Slammer, but I've got some dangerous people after me."

I stepped in and fired up a Lucky Strike. That usually annoyed the Hollywood crowd, but this sap needed me so he didn't say boo.

"The people you're mixed up with are only dangerous if you don't pay them. You make good dough, what's the matter, got a bad habit that needs feeding? The vig too rich for your blood?"

"It's not the money, Mr. Slammer. I have plenty. I borrowed the money under the table to finance a... special project."

"So now you're being blackmailed? What is it, porn? Girl on girl, maybe midgets? A trapeze artist and an endangered animal? Something with nuns? If it's altar boys you can count me out while you're counting your teeth."

"No, nothing like that. You see, I have a certain reputation to maintain. My movies make a lot of money, but I've always wanted to do more."

"More?" I said, taking a long pull from my hip flask. Now I was getting interested. Not as interested as I was in girl on girl porn, but it was only 10 am. There was always lunchtime.

"Let's face it, Mr. Slammer, I make lowest common denominator action flicks. Tripe for the masses. That pays the bills, but you see, I've always want to make a real movie. Something Merchant-Ivory, something classy! You know, *Remains of the Day* rather than *Remains in the Hay*."

"I saw that one. Not bad, but trust me, a double barreled twelve gauge does way more damage than that to a gymnast."

"I'll take your word for it. Anyway, I'm at the point in my career where I'm concerned about my legacy."

"What's with you Hollywood types? Making buckets of money and doing the horizontal hula with every starry eyed chorine with a dream isn't enough? You have to make 'art', too? Why don't you just take up an annoying cause like the rest of your pinko pals?"

"I want to do something I can be proud of, that my children can be proud of, something they can brag about in therapy! But if it got out that I was making a quality movie I'd be box office poison. That's why I'm being blackmailed. I borrowed the money to hide the fact that I was behind the project."

"And now you're behind the eight ball. If I've seen it once, I've seen it a hundred times." I hadn't even seen it once, but I had to let this ham cure the way I wanted him to.

"Can you help me, Mr. Slammer?" He handed me a sheet of paper with a name on it. I knew the guy. A piece of genetic diarrhea named Flosser. Ironic, as it was something he never did. And bathing was something he reserved for special occasions, too, like the Bicentennial. I got back in my Desoto and went to have a heart to heart. The guard at the gate was still in dreamland, so I let myself out.

I found Flosser in a dive on Hollywood Boulevard. The creatures of the shadows who lurked there weren't the product of broken dreams, they were the product of broken condoms. Flosser was at the bar nursing a beer. I sidled up to him and ordered a shot of the good stuff. In a joint like that, it was something gardeners sprayed on the azaleas to kill aphids.

"I didn't know you had any brain cells left to kill, Flosser", I said. He looked at me the wrong way, which was in my direction.

"You want something, flatfoot?"

That was all the excuse I needed. In a flash I was all over him like white on an albino. "First of all, a flatfoot's a cop, which I'm not any more, so I don't have to worry about little things like the Miranda Warning or finding the next of kin." I grabbed the lapels of his greasy polyester suit and gave him a taste of the bar with plenty of broken shot glass as a chaser.

"You're making trouble for one of my clients, and that makes trouble for you." I kicked him hard enough to make his testicles show up on a throat culture. "You're gonna forget all about Tom Tellmark, savvy?" I grabbed him by his white belt and cheap shirt and threw him through the front window. The light pouring in sent the regulars scuttling like cockroaches, which was an insult to the roaches. I went out to see if my talk had made a difference. It did, all right. He was impaled on a parking meter, gurgling out his last fetid breath. Just then, Lt. Breeks, my old partner from the force, happened by.

"What happened here, Spike? Another suicide?"

"Sorry about the parking meter, Breeks, but this wankstain was leaning on a client of mine. I can't go into detail, but he needed to see the light, and it was too dark in there."

Just then a meter maid came by. "I can't read this meter. I'd better give the guy a ticket just to be on the safe side."

"I guess his time's expired, eh, Spike?" Breeks quipped. Even the meter maid had to laugh at that one, and they weren't known for their sense of humor.

"Just earning a living, Breeks", I said, lighting up a smoke. "Why don't you have someone hose off the sidewalk while I tell my client the good news?"

I got back in my car and headed back to the studio. The guy at the gate just waved me through. Fast learner. I got to Tellmark's bungalow and was surprised to see the door wide open. Tellmark was inside, packing a suitcase and humming.

"Ah, Mr. Slammer, come in!" He seemed pretty chipper for a guy who still had a price on his noggin. I sensed something was up, something I wasn't going to like.

"I take it you took care of our friend Flosser? Don't be surprised, Mr. Slammer. I figured you'd send him to the morgue. That's why I hired you."

Dawn was breaking and I didn't like the view. "So, it was a set-up?"

"Of course it was. Some kind of acting, wasn't it? I wanted

Emotional Chaos

Flosser dead and you were only too happy to oblige."

I tried to keep my cool as I lit up a smoke. "May I ask why you wanted Flosser dead, other than to improve the gene pool?"

"Certainly", he said, cracking open a bottle of designer water. Actors always love the sound of their own voice. "Flosser was backing my movie, all right, but he wanted to bigger a slice of the profits than I was willing to give. So I decided to cut him out, permanently. With your help, of course. It's all about the points in this business, Slammer." I noticed that he'd dropped the "Mister".

I didn't like being played by anyone. "The points, you say?"

"That's right. Now if you'll excuse me, I think your work is done."

"No", I said, closing the door. "This script is still in development."

The next morning I was in a coffee shop on Wiltshire when Breeks came in. "Still warming your joe with Jack Daniels, Spike?" he said, sitting down and ordering some eggs. "Say, did you hear about Tom Tellmark, the actor? Drowned in his own toilet. The M.E. ruled it accidental. Figured he slipped while doing yoga, or pilates, or whatever those movie stars do these days."

"Yeah, that's a real shame", I said without looking up from my hash, "I hear he had a good movie coming out".

THE RIGHT STIFF

How many of us yearn for the good old days of aviation, when pilots with "The Right Stuff" "Pushed the Envelope" and frequently "Augered In"? The stories of those exciting times have become legendary, yet many of those fearless men are all but forgotten. Sure, the astronauts got all the press, but what about the nameless, faceless (some quite literally) test pilots that never got the glory? Today we honor those neglected heroes.

Our first forgotten hero is Captain Eddie "Spats" Spittle (U.S. Army Air Corps, ret.). A decade before the record breaking flights in the high desert of the southwest, long before Alan Shepard and John Glenn, Captain Spittle claims to have made history. We spoke with him at his cabin in Brooklyn, where, now retired from his job as a roach poison tester, Spittle spends his days reminiscing and making hats out of tinfoil.

"I was the first man in space! I did it in 1941!"

We were skeptical, but let him go on.

"I see you're skeptical, but I'll go on. It was early December, 1941. I gassed up my old T-22 Flying Scrapheap, and took off into the Wild Blue. That's what we called it in those day, the 'Wild Blue'. None of this candy-ass 'Wild Blue Yonder' stuff! That was for the guys who spent the war in New Jersey, if you catch my drift! Anyway, I decided to see how high she'd go, so I gunned the engine and headed straight up. After a long while things started floatin' around the cockpit. That's what we called it in those days, 'the cockpit'. It was dark, I could see stars and I had to use the oxygen tank to breathe. I realized then that I was in outer space. That's what we called it in those days, 'outer space'. I was the first guy to go there, and should have been famous, but the next day the Japs bomber Pearl Harbor, and everybody forgot what I did."

And speaking of the war, World War II created many aviation

heroes. Some are the stuff of legend, some are lost to the mists of time. One such man is Sir Geoffrey Bosco-Loomis, a fighter pilot in the Battle of Britain. Realizing that the island nation was facing overwhelming odds against the might of Nazi Germany, he devised a unique plan to save ammunition. He explained it in a 1941 BBC radio interview:

"I hit upon the idea of aiming my Spitfire at the German bombers and leaping out at the last minute. The plane would then crash into the bomber, taking out Jerry before he knew what hit him!"

But, as he was using up a plane a day, his plan was never popular with his superiors. Like many brave young men in those dark days, his life ended too soon. He died in 1942 when the Air Minister shot him.

After the war, hotshot pilots headed to Muroc Field (later Edwards Air Force Base) in the high desert, where every kind of experimental plane was being flown and every aviation record was being challenged. Plus, the chili was good. One of the boldest, the bravest, the most fearless and the most blase (although real test pilots NEVER used terms like blase. Using words like that, as well as "precious", "exquisite", "scrumptious" and "parasol" would get you immediately branded as an outsider) was Colonel Malcolm "Chuckles" Crossfingers. Known throughout the flying fraternity as "The Man Who Laughed at Unpleasant Conditions", Chuck Yeager once said of him, "If you told him to fly through a lightnin' storm headlong into a mesa, he'd do it. He was kinda stupid like that." Another ex-test pilot, Michael Collins, put it more succinctly. "The guy was strictly psycho city. When he was flying we routinely evacuated the base". Before his retirement in 1964, Crossfingers held the records for most cockpit canopies damaged (he felt that "real pilots don't blow the canopy before punching out That's for guys who spent the war in New Jersey, if you catch my drift!", so he never once did so, even though he was forced to eject 437 times. We think that explains a lot), most parachutes eaten (although no one else was even in the running for that one), most civilian aircraft shot down and most outsiders beaten up for using the word "exquisite". Today he spends his time shooting paper clips at passing airliners.

In today's world of computers, heads up cockpit displays, satellite communication and high-tech weaponry, maybe there's no use for seat of the pants pilots like Spittle, Bosco-Loomis and Crossfingers. An era has passed, never to return. Now that I think about it, it's probably for the best.

THE GREAT WHITE WAY

People frequently come up to me on the street and ask, "Say, what's new on Broadway this season?" Invariable I respond, "How the hell should I know? Get away from me, you strange person, before I beat you senseless with this kielbasa!" But, given the frequency of the question and the price of kielbasa these days, I thought I'd look into it. I'm here to report that The Great White Way is as meaty, beaty, big and bouncy as ever. Let's look at some of the blockbusters lighting up the theatre scene:

The hottest new musical of the season is *Pluck!*, which Andrew Lloyd Webber hopes will do for poultry what *Cats* did for felines. Starring a bunch of unknowns who aren't at ALL of questionable sexual orientation. Get that RIGHT out of your mind.

Crocodile Dundee star Paul Hogan is back in *The Wombat King*, also starring Linda Kozlowski, Olivia Newton-John and Yahoo Serious as the Prime Minister of Australia.

And don't miss the musical version of *Apollo 13* starring Nathan Lane, Mandy Patinkin and Matthew Broderick as the ill fated crew, Mark Hamill as Ken Mattingly and Glenn Close as Gene Kranz. The show features such memorable tunes as "Rocket to the Moon", "Houston, We Have a Problem" and "Maneuvering Thrusters On!"

In the wake of the success of *Riverdance*, we have *Beyond the Pale*, the all albino step dancing troupe, and although the Richard Nixon bioplay *Sunset at Yorba Linda* has closed after a successful five year run, fans of our 37th president will enjoy *I, Richard* with Derek Jacobi in the title role, Ian McKellan as Bob Haldeman, Patrick Stewart as John Ehrlichman, Hugh Grant as John Dean and the late John Gielgud as John Mitchell. Although the part of Spiro Agnew hasn't been cast, the Broadway rumor mill says the smart money is on either Robin Williams or Swamp Thing.

Emotional Chaos

Of course, it wasn't all success on Broadway this season. The blockbuster musical *Ishtar!*, based on the Warren Beatty/Dustin Hoffman movie was the most expensive flop since *Schindler's List on Ice*, and *An Evening with Gilbert Gottfried* closed after one rehearsal.

I've been thinking of pitching the idea of an existential version of *The Sound of Music*. Existential musicals are hot right now (look at *The Non-Producers*). I mean, wasn't *The Sound of Music* ALWAYS a metaphor for man's struggle against totalitarianism and a parallel to the rise of Nazi Germany? Or was that *The Music Man*? Anyway, by changing the names of all the characters to "Horst", replacing the Rodgers and Hammerstein score with Kraftwerk and having all the actors in black leotards on a totally black set covered with broken glass, I think I captured the essence of what the writer MEANT to say! Here's an excerpt:

The scene: a blackened room, somewhere in Austria in the late 1930s.

Horst 1: "I'm Horst, the new governess. Fate has brought me here for reasons only the fathomless mind of God can OW!! I've cut myself! There's glass everywhere!"

Horst 2: "Life is pain. Pain is life. All this glass glitters like the broken dreams of the Bourgeois."

Horst 1: "We'd better not sit down, then!"

Horst 2: "Glass is my bed. I bleed, I cry, often I seek medical attention... only through pain can we know we're alive!"

Horst 3: (to the hypnotic thrum of *Kraftwerk*): "*Alive. Alive. The hills are alive! Alive. Alive. The hills are alive!*"

Horst 2: "I must join the Austrian Navy. I can do nothing else. Free will is a cruel illusion."

Horst 3: "*Alive. Alive. The hills are alive! Alive. Alive. The hills are alive!*"

Horst 2: "Take care of the children, Horst, Horst, Horst, Horst,

Emotional Chaos

Horst and especially my darling little Horst!"

Horst 1: "As much as anyone can care in a pointless universe."

The children, Horst, Horst, Horst, Horst, Horst and Horst come on stage and join Horst 3 in singing "*Alive. Alive. The hills are alive! Alive. Alive. The hills are alive!*"

I can see it now! It would make a perfect vanity piece for Julia Roberts and Keanu Reeves! I'll have my people call your people.

WHO YA GONNA CALL?

It amazes me how many "ghost hunter" shows there are on TV these days, considering that they never find anything conclusive. They generally consist of a bunch of Cockney con artists (or other reliable sources) reacting to nothing while bathed in eerie infrared light.

"What's that?" one will say, glowing red eyes looking around furtively.

"My God! It's 5 degrees colder in the basement than it was in the kitchen!" says the second. Before the audience can figure out that's perfectly normal another one says "Did you see that light streak? Let's show the replay!" Which they do, and yes there is a light streak, but it could be anything from a reflection to bad camera work.

And, of course, there's the recordings:

"Okay, we left the recorder here overnight, let's see what it picked up!"

Recorder: HISSSSSSS blurble HISSSSSSSS"

"Did you hear that? It clearly said "I died in 1936!"

So, being naturally skeptical, we did some research on the paranormal. We had questions; what are ghosts? Why do they stay on this Earthly plane? Do they get a senior discount?

Here are some actual cases that may prove the existence of ghosts:

In 1968 Merle Crowder of Bassmouth, Florida bought a house that had previously been a mortuary, slaughterhouse, slave market, brothel and used car lot. Oh yes, it was also the scene of the infamous Bassmouth Manatee Massacre, which needs no introduction. When his family moved in strange things started to happen. They thought it was haunted, but no one believed them. Except the neighbors, who burned the house down.

Emotional Chaos

On a cold December day in 1973 Thor Mucilage of Muncie, Indiana killed his entire family with a rolled up copy of Vanity Fair. Since then, no one in Muncie can read Vanity Fair without feeling a cold chill run down their spine. Of course, few people in Muncie read Vanity Fair, it's really not a problem.

Even people who don't know the dark history of Bleak Outlook Cottage in Rockport, Massachusetts feel the presence of something terribly evil when they enter. It's the owner, Peabody J. Whiffle, who no one wants to visit anyway.

Upon hearing about this story Mercy Mee of Galveston, Texas wrote to us about a strange thing that happened to her one night:

"I was strangling my husband Lars when I heard a voice saying 'Go the distance!'. I thought it was a sign, but it turned out that *Field of Dreams* was on TV in the other room. But I figured 'what the hell', and finished the job. I've never been bothered by evil spirits since! Of course, I never was before, Lars just had to go."

The people of Starkweather, Maine tell the story of a strange light that they see in the sky at night. After driving all that way to investigate, it turned out to be the lights of Portland some sixty miles away. Ah, that dry Yankee humor!

Undeterred, we then traveled to that hotbed of ghostly activity, Gettysburg, Pennsylvania. That terrible battle in July of 1863 saw over 50,000 soldiers dead, wounded or missing. Many think this horrific suffering makes Gettysburg one of the most haunted places in America. Local resident Otto Salmon spends much of his time roaming the battlefields in search of ghosts. He has many stories to tell. We met him at the Wailing Pickett Tavern for drinks.

"Yep", he said, "I've seen things, heard things, felt things you can't imagine!" He took a deep draw from his bucket of scotch and leaned over. "Once, I clearly saw the ghost of General Ulysses S. Grant walking across Little Round Top!"

We pointed out to him that General Grant was nowhere near Gettysburg during the battle. He was adamant.

Emotional Chaos

"It was Grant, alright! He looked right at me! Or should I say... through me!"

We assured him he shouldn't and let him go on, as we could write off the bar tab on our taxes.

"And another time a column of Union troops marched right through my rutabaga patch!"

We pointed out that according to the local papers it was a group of Civil War reenactors (the 28th Massachusetts specifically, but you didn't hear it from me) and that they were merely lost. Once again, he was adamant.

"This place is lousy with ghosts! If they could vote Abe Lincoln would still be in the White House!" With that he passed out in his nachos.

So, are you convinced? The next time you hear a creak when no one's there, see a fleeting motion out of the corner of your eye or see a strange light in the woods at night, ask yourself, "What am I doing in the woods this time of night?"

I'm going with alien abduction.

THE FUTURE, AND HOW TO AVOID IT

Ever since the dawn of time, man has endeavored to predict the future:

Early man 1: "Ngghhhh!!!!"

Early man 2: "Hnguuuhh!!!"

After they developed language, things got a little easier:

Not quite as early man 1: "I'm intrigued by what wonders the future holds for us, Og!"

Not quite as early man 2: "Hnguuuhh!!!"

Once everyone got on the same page, predicting the future became big business. By far the most famous oracle was the Oracle at Delphi. Kings and commoners alike climbed Mount Parnassos to seek its wisdom. The Gods spoke through women chosen for their ability to do really creepy *Exorcist*-like voices while delivering the prophecies:

Ancient Greek: "Wise Oracle, I've come all the way from Crete to learn my future!"

Oracle: "When twelve dawns break clear, the chickens shall roost before the Thracian wind!"

Ancient Greek: "Okay. Well, I don't understand it, but you delivered it on such a creepy *Exorcist*-like voice that it must be true. What else can you tell me?"

Oracle: "All is known by the Gods. What is uttered by the Oracle is the whisper of those divine voices, and unto the curious who seek the infinite knowledge of the Oracle, no refunds shall be granted."

Another famous visionary of ancient times was Joseph. As the Bible tells us, Joseph got a job as a slave in Egypt, which was a rapidly growing field but without much chance for advancement. The ancient Egyptians believed that dreams were full of powerful messages about the future, and those with the ability to interpret them were respected, revered and invited to all the best parties. Joseph developed quite a reputation as an interpreter of dreams and visions, although his average at picking the chariot race winners was only so-so. Still, his talents came to the attention of the Pharaoh, who summoned him to the pyramid to interpret a particularly strange and foreboding dream:

Pharaoh: "Last night I dreamed seven emaciated cows ate seven fat cows, and seven dry ears of corn ate seven healthy ears!"

Joseph: "BWAHAHAHA!!!!! Uh, oh, I'm sorry. You were serious about that? Okay, let's see. I'd say it means that Egypt will have seven years of plenty, followed by seven years of famine and drought. It would be a good idea to stockpile grain for the next seven years so we can get through the lean times. And it's probably not too early to invest in Microsoft stock."

Not only did Joseph's predictions come true, earning him great esteem in the eyes of the Pharaoh, but he also got a cushy job as grain collector. There's a lesson there for all of us.

Perhaps the most famous of all seers was Nostradamus. A French physician and astrologer who lived from 1503-1566, Nostradamus was known even in his own time as a man who could see the future. He wrote in what were called "quatrains", a form of prophetic poetry that was as vague as it was obtuse:

Sitting alone at night in secret study; it is placed on the brass tripod.

A slight flame comes out of the emptiness and

Makes successful that which should not be believed in vain.

Believers point to his quatrains and say that he predicted World War I, the rise of Hitler and Nazi Germany, World War II, the atomic bomb, Nutra-Sweet and the inexplicable popularity of Adam Sandler. Although his predictions were pretty vague, and could as easily refer to Groucho Marx as Karl Marx, people put great stock in his premonitions. Some say that his predictions about the end of the world will prove the nonbelievers wrong once and for all, but, if the world ends, who'll be around to gloat?

Another visionary was Edgar Cayce, known as "The Sleeping Prophet". This is a good job if you can get it, as you never even have to get out of bed.

Believer: "My husband went out for a paper and never came back! Will he return? And, if he ran off with the bimbo who runs the soda fountain at the drugstore, is there a plague of boils in his future?"

Cayce: "Zzzzzzzzzzz!"

Believer: "Can I take that as a yes?"

Cayce: "Znnnnnx!"

Believer: "I'll let myself out."

An almost forgotten psychic was an Englishman known only as "Cairo". Cairo's most famous prediction warned Lord Canarvon that opening the tomb of King Tutankhamen was a big mistake, even worse than the time he stuck his finger in the light socket (Cairo had warned against that, too, earning Canarvon's trust and confidence). His average slipped after that, and he eventually went into the wholesale plumbing supply business.

Can the future be known? Is it immutable, or with knowledge can we control our destinies? I think Edgar Cayce said it best: "Znnnnnx!"

MAIL CALL

Today we're going to dip into the old mail bag to answer questions from you, the great unwashed... I mean general public. This is a time honored literary device, used mostly when the author can't think of anything interesting to write about, or spent the night drinking and is now facing both a deadline and a hangover. Shakespeare famously exploited this technique in *The Podiatrist of Sutton*, Act II, Scene III:

Bongo: "Whence twather in the door'yard prevailed, dids't thou ponder where ponces flame?"

Frostcake: "Let us quibble not, nor scenery chew! Rather into the missives shall we dip, and from the canvas maw withdraw a query! Lebron of Blankstare writes, 'Prithee, what's the story with Hamlet?' A fair question! Surely he is with issues plagued, but I would recommend him dealing with it."

And, of course, in Hemingway's *The Sun Also Rises*, The narrator, Jake Barnes, begins the story by talking about his past to Robert Cohn, an aspiring writer. This gets pretty boring by chapter 3, so Barnes, a newspaper correspondent, decides to liven up the action by "responding to a sample of the dispatches from Paris"...

"Dear Jake: I met a young bullfighter in Madrid. I'm inflamed with passion, but ever since I lost my generation I can't bring myself to care. Signed: Wanda"

"Dear Wanda: Who gives a damn? I need a drink."

And so on. So, without further ado, let's check out the mail. After all, who are we to argue with such great writers?

Enid Gargoyle of Stutter, Alberta writes, *"Have you ever thought of doing a column devoted to Jello molds? I have the largest collection of Jello molds outside of Nebraska, and always enjoy good Jello mold talk!"*

Dear Enid: No. But, by an extraordinary coincidence, our next letter is about Jello molds.

Jasper Wyoming, of Anubisburg, Pennsylvania writes: "*I sell factory second Jello molds. You know, the kind that will still make a fine dessert, but aren't up to Jello's strict standards. I mean, with a little whipped cream no one will know, and you'll save a bundle over so-called 'perfect' Jello molds. Oh, yes, we also sell factory second swizzle sticks, but that's a story for another day!*"

Indeed it is, Jasper, indeed it is...

Otis Sanguine, of Hellbound, Mississippi writes, "*Just yesterday, I drove my Chevy to the levee, and not only wasn't the levee dry, but the mud sucked my Chevy right in. I don't care about the car, but I'd really like to recover the* Paladin *lunchbox my wife was holding in her lap when the car sank. Anyway, can I sue Don McLean?*"

Well, Otis, we think you have a strong case against Don McLean. The only problem is, he hasn't had a hit in decades, so it might be tough to get a judgement. We suggest suing Chevrolet instead, for not including a warning about driving off levees in the owner's manual.

Bosco Snapple writes: "*I think it's time we recognized the enormous contribution to the science of optics and astronomy made by those great 17th century Dutch scientists Aanders Flemloosen and Naaked van der Slugg. They've been neglected too long, overshadowed by flashier, or 'sexier' if you will, scientists like Newton and Leeuwenhoek! I think they're just as important, and I'll personally strangle anyone who disagrees!*"

Lest you think Bosco is just some run of the mill nut, you should know that he's Associate Professor of Theoretical Lunacy at Greenblatt Junior College (formerly Greenblatt Junior College and Idiot Depository) and holder of the prestigious Norman Bates Chair in Irrationality. A run of the mill nut would be someone like Basil Zapf of New Palsy, New York:

"*These days people are always talking about 'values' and 'what's important'. Well, I have MY priorities straight! For me*

Emotional Chaos

the most important things in my life are full contact yodeling, followed by baseball, my family, eating lard, moose taunting, watching videos of classic test patterns and twisting small animals. If more people had their lives together the world wouldn't be the way it is, I tell you!"

No arguments from us, Basil. The rest of you, keep those cards and letters coming!

EINE KLEINE BEATDOWN
A Spike Slammer Mystery

I was sitting in my office on Sunset, flipping cards into a fedora and killing off my second bottle of Jim Beam. I hadn't had a case in two weeks and Lola had expensive tastes in eateries. Just then there was a knock on the door. Hesitant, quick, the knock of a sap who was in over his head and needed pulling out from the deep end, although I only did mouth to mouth with dames. I slipped my .45 out of its holster and put it under the Racing Form. "The doorknob ain't gonna twist itself, bright eyes." I said. "Come on in."

A tall, thin man with a beak like a buzzard and a freshly shaved head came in. I could tell he wasn't from around here, only because he didn't have anything nasty covering his shoes.

"Good Morning, Mr. Slammer" he said in a thick German accent. I parted the blinds and glanced out. "If you say so. What can I do for you, Fritz?"

"Hans. Hans Zaftig, late of Munich."

I was less than impressed. "What brings you to L.A.? Looking for a jeweled falcon?"

The reference went right over his melon. "Nein, uh, no. Nothing of the sort. May I sit?" I nodded and poured a shot. "Drink"?

"No, thank you. Ten is a bit early in the morning for me, but don't let me stop you."

I didn't need permission from Erich von Stroheim to drink in my own office but I let it go. I belted down the booze and got down to business. "What's burning your schnitzel, Klaus?"

"I need to find a man. A fellow German who owes me money."

"It must be a load of Deutchmarks to make you follow him all the way to L.A."

I never liked doing business with krauts, especially since that incident in Bonn. I showed him the foot long scar on my thigh. It was easy enough, I already had my pants down and wasn't about to pull them up for some goose stepper. "I picked this up the last time I trusted a German." I didn't go into detail, but it was a case I had a while ago that started in Zurich. I followed a fraulein named Hildegarde all the way to Bonn. She looked innocent enough, but backed into a corner she made Ilsa, She-Wolf of the SS look like Heidi. Long story short, I gave her an Eva Braun facial with my .45, which pretty much ended the case.

"So, what makes you think this mook is in tinseltown?"

"Let me start at the beginning. I'm a diamond merchant. High end stones for only the finest jewelers in Europe."

"I'm losing interest, Adolf. Get to the point."

"I met a man named Schlapp on the Schmutzigstrasse who said he had some fine stones from South Africa. The sort of diamonds that have no papers, if you follow me."

"I know about you krauts and your papers. Go on." I poured another shot.

"I brought a substantial amount of money to a cafe in Misthaufen to complete the transaction. When Schlapp didn't show I became nervous and left. No sooner did I reach my car when I was struck from behind and rendered unconscious. When I awoke the money was gone."

I nodded. The 'old lure the mark to a public place, stand him up and when he's alone douse his lights with a pipe'. I've had to use that one on clients who'd rather cough up blood than cough up my fee. Either way works for me.

Zaftig continued. "I made some inquiries and apparently Schlapp had pulled the same trick on some others in my profession. He knew, of course, that we couldn't go to the police."

"So the Gestapo couldn't help you. Why L.A.?"

"I did some research and heard of a similar crime taking place here. A few discreet inquiries lead me to believe that it was Schlapp."

"Sounds interesting. Okay, I'll look into it. But I get paid in cash, U.S. greenbacks, not hot rocks, savvy, Heinrich?"

"Ja, yes, I understand."

"And I do it my way. I don't follow orders."

He slipped a billfold from his jacket pocket and pulled out five crisp hundreds. "Here is what I know. Schlapp was seen in the jeweler's district. He's a stout man with a slight limp, a Prussian accent and a polished bearing, not at all like a common verbrecher, criminal, ja?"

I picked up the bills and his calling card. "I'll let you know what I find out. You won't be upset if I have to do a little arm twisting, will you?"

"Do what is necessary, Mr. Slammer. You'll be handsomely rewarded."

I went down to the jeweler's district that afternoon to ask around to see if anyone had seen anyone resembling Schlapp. Jewelers are a pretty insular bunch, and they know all the players in the game, the ones on the level, the ones on the take and the ones on the lam. A stone cutter named Narrischkeit owed me a favor. Business involving his wife, his brother-in-law, a midget and some non-kosher blintzes. If I heard it once, I heard it a thousand times...

Narrischkeit had a small shop in the center of the district. He saw me at the door and buzzed me in. "Spike, how long has it been? Come in!"

"Thanks, Moishe. I'm looking for information. Seen any Germans around here lately? Stocky gimp with good manners?"

"A German with good manners? Now that would stand out! Now that you mention it, Durkhfall had a customer, a German who wanted to sell some diamonds. Good ones, but Durkhfall was suspicious. I mean he looked like a choshever mentsh, you know, respectable, but he something wasn't right. The guy said to call him at the Hotel Fardross if he changed his mind."

"Thanks, Chaim, I owe you one." I left his place and got into my Desoto. The Hotel Fardross was a flop about four blocks away. Nice and private, someplace where no one would look for you. I staked out the place and sure enough Schlapp came out around 5:00. He was stocky, had a limp and dressed with class. He looked nervous and clutched his case to his chest like it was a dame and he'd just done six years in solitary. I followed him to a coffee shop on Wiltshire. I decided that a direct approach was best. I went into the cafe, picking up a steak knife from the counter. I sat down across from him, looking directly into his dingy yellow eyes.

"You Schlapp?"

"Ja, Johann Schlapp, diamond broker. And you are?"

"Name's Slammer. I'm a shamus and my client says you owe him some scratch."

"I don't understand. I'm supposed to owe someone money?"

"You got it. I hear you run a diamond scam. I bet you've got a load of hot merchandise in that satchel. Mind if I have a peek?"

He was reluctant to give up the case so I drove the knife through his left hand. When your hand is pinned to a table you tend get cooperative real fast. I took the case and unsnapped the flap. Inside was a blue velvet bag with enough diamonds to give Elizabeth Taylor a stroke. There was something hypnotic about the glittering gems, almost enough to make me forget Schlapp's screaming. I got back to business.

"You took some green off a guy named Zaftig in Misthaufen, remember? Smacked his casaba with a sap and dashed with the Deutschmarks."

"I sell diamonds! Okay, they don't have paperwork, but I can sell them cheaper that way! My clients don't complain!"

"That's because they're face down in the street. It's bad enough you're selling blood diamonds, but you have to cheat the marks, too? That bratwurst don't cook, Wolfgang! I tell you what, give my client back his money and I won't finish the steak knife stigmata!"

"I have no money! Take the diamonds, they're worth more than what I took from Zaftig!"

I picked up the bag and stashed it in my pocket. I walked out and flipped the waitress a rock the size of a cue ball. "This should induce amnesia when the cops arrive, right, doll?" There was no argument from her.

When I got back to my office Zaftig was waiting for me. I told him what happened and unlocked the door. When I turned around I was staring into the muzzle of a Luger.

"I'll take those diamonds, Herr Slammer."

I was putting two and two together and any way you did the math I was a goner.

"I knew you'd lead me to Schlapp. So predictable, you Americans!"

I handed him the bag, spilling some of the diamonds onto the floor. When he looked down I flicked a diamond that I had palmed into his face. That was enough to get him to flinch, and when he did I grabbed the gat, spun him around and sent him sailing through the window in a hail of glass and gemstones. It was three stories down; when I got there Breeks, my old partner from the force was waiting.

"Look at all these diamonds, Spike! When they hose 'em off I bet there'll be a million bucks worth!"

I snapped open my Zippo and torched a Camel. "Gives new meaning to the expression 'blood diamonds', eh, Breeks?"

Emotional Chaos

CIRCUS OF THE DAMNED

"The Family Circus" as envisioned by Stephen King. Or at least as we envision Stephen King would envision it.

Thel had never noticed that nothing had changed since 1956. It wasn't until Barfy spoke to her that she realized that time was frozen, that it was still 1956, always 1956. How much time had passed? She couldn't say. Then the dotted lines began to appear. They crisscrossed the living room, the yard, the street. They were everywhere, but no one else could see them, or would admit seeing them. Where did they come from? No one else seemed to notice or care. Were they in denial, or was it something more sinister, the same force that froze time, trapping her in an Eisenhower-era Hell? It was always "Not Me" or the mysterious wraith "Ida Know". But someone knew. Barfy, the family dog, knew. And he imparted his wisdom to Thel, but like all things, it came with a price. It was a price she was willing to pay to escape the nightmare. No price was too great, she thought, as she sat in the 1950s modern living room, watching the static on the Philco console TV, listening to the clock tick and fingering the handle of the shovel that felt almost weightless in her hands. Time had no meaning, nothing mattered. Barfy assured her, though, that once it was done she'd be free.

She heard the school bus stop out front and soon Jeffy came tumbling into the house. He noticed the shovel, but didn't say anything. Was that blood on its blade? It was probably just mud, Jeffy thought. He'd always had an active imagination.

"Where's Billy and Dolly?" he asked. They usually came home on the earlier bus with the grammar school kids. Jeffy was still in kindergarten after all these years, so he took the later bus.

"They're in the back yard with Daddy", Thel heard herself say, "Come, let's join them." She was amazingly calm. It was just as Barfy had said it would be. Soon it would all be done.

They went out to the patio beyond the car port into the back

85

Emotional Chaos

yard. Thel had enjoyed gardening ever since she'd planted a Victory Garden during the Second World War. Her husband, Bill, had served in the war, but for some reason was still only 35. It's funny, she thought, how she never noticed something so obvious before.

"Where did that scarecrow come from?" Jeffy asked. "Maybe he's guardin' the garden!"

Thel felt her hands tighten on the shovel's smooth wooden handle. Yes, Jeffy was only five, but it seemed like she'd been listening to his sickeningly cute quips... how long? It seemed like fifty years. It was a good thing the scarecrow was facing away from the house. Jeffy mustn't see its true nature, no, not until they reached the garden. The garden and freedom.

"That looks like Daddy's favorite shirt the scarecrow's wearing" Jeffy said brightly, unaware of what was to come, "Except for that big red paint stain. I remember when Dolly accidentally got paint on PJ's pajamas!"

Thel remembered it well. Once again the denial. Once again, "Not Me" and "Ida Know" were to blame. Again and again and again. "Yes, paint. That's why it's on the scarecrow. Daddy won't be need... won't want to wear a shirt with a big stain on it".

They reached the garden, where the neat rows of plants had been replaced by freshly turned earth. Jeffy wondered why the garden was all dug up, why there was a big hole where the tomatoes had begun to blossom. Mommy was so proud of her garden. Maybe "Not Me" and "Ida Know" had once again worked their mischief and blamed the kids. No one believed they were real, but Jeffy, Billy, Dolly and PJ knew they were. Where were his brothers and sister, anyway?

Suddenly, terribly, his questions were answered, He looked in horror at the hole. He could see Dolly's red dress half covered by the dark, rich smelling soil, her sightless eyes staring up into the sky. Billy's half buried body lay next to her, the blood still oozing from his scalp. Jeffy couldn't see PJ's small form, completely

Emotional Chaos

obscured by Dolly's corpse, covered in mulch.

"What happened? Who did this?" he cried, transfixed by the sight, the unbridled horror, unable to turn away, too scared to run.

"Not Me!" said Thel. It was the last thing Jeffy heard before a blow from the shovel sent him headlong into eternal blackness. It was over. She was free at last. She turned to Barfy, who had tagged along and was now looking down into the hole with her.

"Say something cute now, you oval headed freak", Barfy sneered.

NOT JUST THE FACTS, MA'AM

I want to be a TV cop.

With the exception of the dozens of *Law and Order* franchises (most of which seem to have starred Chris Noth at some point), where most of the cops act like cops in manner and dress and the lawyers act like lawyers right down to the slime trail, many TV cops:

Drive cool, cherry vintage cars that always have whatever they need in the trunk and never need to stop for gas. And no matter how many bullets get shot into them they're fixed and ready to go by the next day. I wonder how many mechanics keep a supply of tail lights for a 1968 Camaro in stock? Maybe they know a steady customer when they see one.

They can transfer from one city or department to another without any loss of rank, seniority, pension status, etc. whenever they need a change of venue because they shot the wrong guy, crossed their boss once too often or just couldn't handle the pressure of the job.

They never have an unsolved case, except for one way back when that still haunts them. Of course, they finally solve it, unless the show is cancelled without notice.

When off duty they hang out in bars where the bartender is a colorful character, a hot blonde or a grizzled ex-cop. They also behave in colorful, eccentric ways, either playing the blues, exotic animal barbecuing, competitive yodeling or something else that real people rarely do.

They wear stylish yet slightly rebellious clothes, which, of course, annoys their superiors. They also leave their badges clipped to their belts all the time because it looks so cool, although it's a dead giveaway on an undercover assignment.

Speaking of which, they also go undercover a lot and can play any role better than Brad Pitt. Some are realistic undercover gigs;

drug dealer, fence, hit man, but you know a show is on the down-hill slide when one of the characters goes undercover as a stripper. Especially if it's Detective Sipowicz, but the less said about that the better. Along those lines, I remember watching an episode of CSI where we're told that a member of the team was a stripper before she became a detective. Repeatedly. But, what else can an exotic dancer do when she gets too old to swing around a pole besides join an elite police unit? If I've heard it once I've heard it a dozen times. On CSI, anyway.

Of course, it's not uncommon for them to give up colorful and lucrative careers to become a cop. "I can't believe you gave up being head of neurosurgery at Princeton-Plainsboro Hospital and Poet Laureate of New Jersey to become a cop!" The grizzled ex-cop bartender marvels as he pours a straight bourbon (they never get drunk, either, no matter how much booze the pour down their maws to relieve the pressure of the job).

"I just felt I had to give back." The cop replies, never mentioning that being a rookie patrolman pays a lot less than being a brain surgeon, but hey, that's the price you pay when you feel you have to give back. I have no idea what being Poet Laureate of New Jersey pays, if anything.

They shoot guns that never need to be reloaded or cleaned and can be tossed around without sustaining any damage. And the backup piece in their ankle holster can stop a moose despite apparently weighing as much as a child's squirt gun. And when they shoot, they either shoot to kill or inflict a flesh wound. They sometimes get shot themselves, but no matter, there's no gunshot wound so serious that it can't be treated by putting your arm in a sling. Plus you get to exchange witty yet sexually charged banter with the hot young Emergency Room doctor. They also banter with the sassy yet world weary coroner who's seen it all and can figure out the cause of death even if the only body part left is a shred of small intestine, but it never goes anyplace.

They only see their ex-wives to exchange acrid banter and

perhaps drop off some barbecued giraffe for the kids so they know they still have a father who wants to shield them from the ugliness he sees every day. And while they never get too close to anyone, they generally date hot soccer moms with smart aleck kids who are wise beyond their years, so it's no wonder their wives left them. That and the pressure of the job.

THE PLAY'S THE THING

Like most humorists, there's a part of me that wants to be taken seriously as a writer, to produce the next Great American Novel, to be a celebrated playwright, or at least get invited to the sort of parties that the literati and glitterati attend: the kind with free booze. I wouldn't compare myself to F. Scott Fitzgerald or James Joyce, although I did once try to pass a check using the name Ernest Hemingway. I got caught because the clerk noticed that I didn't have a white beard, a Hemingwayesque swagger and hadn't been dead since 1961. Curse you, A&E's *Biography*!

Anyway, I've faced the fact at this stage in my life that I'll never be lionized like Eugene O'Neill, get to marry Marilyn Monroe like Arthur Miller or have people make Alec Baldwin movies out of my work like David Mamet.

I'm not even a fan of the theatre, which can be a major obstacle to being a great playwright. For example, I've been to approximately four Broadway plays in my life, unless you count *Beatlemania*. I do realize that plays come in several categories, Drama, (*Long Day's Journey into Night*), Musicals (*Chicago*), Comedy (*The Odd Couple*), Musical Comedy (*Spamalot*) and Crimes Against Humanity (*Starlight Express*). To be considered a serious playwright, though, you have to focus on drama. And while I appreciate good drama as well as the next guy, I find that in the American theatre there seems to be little distinction drawn between drama and just plain misery.

Shakespeare, Shaw, Wilde, they could write comedy, drama, tragedy... if they were alive today they'd probably add musicals, screenplays and a rap album, possibly together. But the American tradition is different. I'm sorry, Tennessee "Ernie Ford" Williams was indisputably a top rank talent who could sling a pen like DiMaggio swung a bat, but I just can't relate to his work. When I was growing up, every single person around me wasn't a drunk, drug addict, pervert or emotional cripple. Uncle Nedgar served

Emotional Chaos

all those functions very well, but that's another story. Eugene O'Neill won four Pulitzers and a Nobel Prize writing about his dysfunctional Irish family. My family is only colorfully Thurberesque, so Thurber already beat me to that. That being said, I've decided to wing it and write my own Great American Drama. I call it *Futile Taffy*. Here's the climactic scene where dark family secrets are laid bare (essential in any Great American Drama).

The scene: The living room of a middle class home somewhere in America. Brothers Bip, Lump, Chip and Lothar have gathered for the funeral of their father. It's a time for introspection and assessment.

Bip: "Ever since I was born, women have abandoned me. As early as I could remember, my mother used to leave me at the bus station for days on end. She claimed it was 'a sociology experiment', but as she worked as a taffy puller her whole life, I was skeptical from an early age. That and the fact that she encouraged me to take candy from strangers. After I grew to manhood I fell in love with Catherine. Catherine, the love of my life, sweet Catherine, who died tragically in a falling safe accident in the bloom of youth! I thought I'd never love again, but then at the lowest depth of my grief I met Mirabel. Ah, Mirabel, she of the laughing eyes, which is kind of disturbing if you think about it. Sweet and chaste she was, too chaste to consummate our love. I could respect that, although I began to question her devotion to her purity when she ran off with the Green Bay Packers. Life teaches many lessons, some of them harsh."

Lump: "Is life a lesson or a cautionary tale? Can we ever know the meaning? Is the life of the elk less than accountant in the eyes of God? Do we not all end the same, the long night of oblivion?"

Bip: "No man can truly know a woman!"

Lump: "And what of the elk?"

Chip: "What's with you and elks?"

Bip: "Father once told me that he never loved mother, that his life was a lie. It was the taffy, only the taffy!"

Emotional Chaos

Lump: "The taffy!"

Chip: "Only the taffy!"

Lothar: "I don't have any lines in this scene."

Bip: "Father loved taffy but could not love a woman."

Bip: "Is anyone capable of love? Is love just a metaphor for futility? And where does that leave the taffy in the grand scheme?"

Chip: "See the light fading from the gazebo! We slip into endless night!"

Lump: "Is that an elk eating the shrubs?"

CURTAIN

Now that I've got that, the rest of this puppy will write itself.

BUILD YOURSELF A
PIRATE'S GRAVE

"While excavating for a new house in the weed-grown lot next door, workmen unearthed a surprising maze of caves and trenches. Evidently they had been dug many seasons before because bushes and weeds were growing luxuriantly from the soil spread over the roofs. Considerable grading and no end of fancy language were required before the lot was in shape to build on. But it proved that a well-made cave is about as substantial a clubhouse as a boy can make.

An important feature is the roof construction. This is of semi-trussed design and can be built from old lumber collected in the club members' backyards. It will drain well and keep the cave warm and dry in the meanest kind of weather.

Grade the excavated dirt away from the hole in an even slope. This helps to conceal its location. Piles of dirt would give you away in a hurry, and scouts from that tough gang over on Boiler Avenue would soon have your stronghold listed for future attack.

Save all the flat stones for the fireplace, unless bricks are available. The latter will make a better fireplace, however, without mortar. The roof or ceiling joists should extend at least a foot on each side of the excavation. The ridge support is made up of two two-by-fours laid one on top of the other, as shown in the diagram. The roof boards should be covered with tar paper or old canvas, or in a pinch, several layers of newspapers. At one end of the roof, tack heavy wire screen under the gable, and further protect this with a row of slats set at an angle. These are to partially support large stones placed against them to conceal the vent. If the stones are big enough they will not impede air circulation to any great extent. A trench is dug for the stove-pipe and, when this is laid, covered over again with dirt. Of course, it will be an advantage to have the chimney as far away from the cave as your supply of stove-pipe will permit. However, be sure that the top of the chimney is one or two feet higher than the stove. Otherwise your draft will be sluggish. Stones should be piled around the chimney to hide it, and it wouldn't be a bad idea to throw over the chimney itself some old junk, such as rusty wash-boilers, etc. that will not interfere with draft. In case a potential enemy sees smoke rising he naturally would assume it to be a rubbish fire.

Cover the roof with soil and then spread leaves and brush over it in a natural manner. Next spring new growth will spring up from the seeds thus sown. Dig a drainage trench around the "eaves" and fill with loose brush to hide it."

From "Building a Pirate's Cave"
Hi Sibley
Modern Mechanics, December 1929

The old man sat on the park bench as Jason walked by, engrossed in his video game.

"Gather round, children! I have a story to tell" said the old man.

Jason looked around. "I'm the only one here."

"Don't backtalk sonny! As I said, I have a tale to tell of when I was your age way back when."

What the hell, Jason thought, and sat on the ground to hear the old man's story.

"When I was a boy every street had its gang, and every gang had a clubhouse."

Jason nodded, texting the details of his whereabouts just in case.

"Some were tree houses, some were shacks, but my gang, the South Side Lindys, decided to build a pirate's cave. Why, you ask? The worst gang in town was the Boiler Avenue Gang. They were into all kinds of bad stuff; rigged stickball games, lemonade stand protection rackets, selling counterfeit Jughead hats and forged Roy Hobbs baseball cards. When Ethelred from the Oak Street

Emotional Chaos

Chums got a little too close to the operation everyone knows that Spike and Sluggo took him to the Boiler Room and waterboarded him until he spilled the beans about the location of their clubhouse. He was found dead in Old Man Beasley's peach orchard with what was described as a 'self inflicted slingshot wound to the head'. It was ruled a suicide. Self inflicted slingshot wound, my Aunt Fanny!"

"Your Aunt Fanny did it?"

"None of your sass, Johnny! We all knew the coroner was on the Boiler Gang's payroll. Yep, they were pretty tough!"

"So, they never found your Pirate's Cave?" asked Jason, now mildly interested.

"Well, actually, Joey, it collapsed within a week. What the hell do a bunch of ten year olds know about underground construction? Luckily, I was out buying Moxie, so I was the only survivor. I hooked up with the Maple Street Marauders and never looked back."

The old man was quiet.

"So that's it?" asked Jason.

"Pretty much. Well, run along, Timmy. Your mother will be looking for you!" And with that the old man passed out.

THE HAT BOX MURDERS
An Inspector Blancmange Mystery

It was a leaden gray day in London, during that depressing season when the fog is so thick you can slice it up and serve it with marmalade on toast. We hadn't had a case in over a fortnight, and were suffering the effects of the boredom that our involuntary confinement invariably brought. Blancmange, being in an especially deep torpor, played absently on his tuba, hoping, as always, for some form or murder or intrigue to bring about much needed mental stimulation. Suddenly, there was a knock on the door of our rooms.

"I think you'll find, Broadbeam, that it's Inspector Glucose and, if I'm not mistaken, he'll be wearing pants and carrying an umbrella!"

I answered the door. It was exactly as Blancmange had predicted.

"How did you know, Blancmange?"

"Quite obvious, my dear Broadbeam. You'll recall that the *Times* predicted rain this afternoon, and our friend Glucose hasn't ventured out without trousers since the incident at the schoolyard!"

"Brilliant! Come in, Glucose! What can we do for you?"

Glucose entered, shook out his umbrella and removed his mac and pants. "Good afternoon, gentlemen! I've got a case that's a real poser! You've no doubt read about the singular murder of Sir Ponsonby-Bleek."

"Ah, yes", said Blancmange, rolling a large joint. A beastly habit, marijuana, but it helped him to think. "He was found in a series of hat boxes all across London!"

"Quite right, Blancmange! Upsetting to the haberdashers, I can tell you! The only clue we have is that all the boxes came from the firm of Merkle and Sons, Ltd. of Rummage Road, Chelsea."

Emotional Chaos

"Hat box suppliers to the Crown since 1774!" I interjected.

"The same! A quite respectable firm."

"I say!" I said.

"Intriguing!" said Blancmange from behind a haze of blue smoke, "Pray, go on!"

"According to Ponsonby-Bleek's solicitors, the firm of Pommeroy, Wolfbane, Harker and Cohen, he leaves an estate worth over 2,000,000 pounds! One would think that would be motive enough for murder, but he had no relatives at all, in fact no potential heirs beyond his household staff."

"No relatives at all, Glucose?" I asked. Murder for inheritance was usually a family affair. "Do you recall 'The Case of the Gilded Weasel'? It turned out that Lady Hampstead's long lost cousin had been masquerading as a tree for 27 years, and only appeared at the reading of the will! He was found guilty of her murder and hanged at Dartmoor later that afternoon."

"Quite right, Broadbeam, but Pommeroy, Wolfbane, Harker and Cohen have done a thorough search. Ponsonby-Bleek's parents were killed in a freak blimp accident when he was away at Eton. His elder sister Annoria died of ennui when he was a boy, and his younger brother Nigel died valiantly fighting the Boers in Afghanistan. The only other relative, his Uncle Jack, was eaten by missionaries in the south seas."

"What a tragic family history!"

"Money can't buy happiness, my dear Broadbeam! But back to the case. Ponsonby-Bleek had no relatives, no enemies, and rarely wore hats! We've spoken to everyone even remotely connected to the case, but have met with nothing but dead ends. We have most of a body, but without a motive this crime has The Yard baffled!"

"Motive, indeed!" said Blancmange. "Let me ponder this, Glucose. In the meantime, gather all the servants and his solicitors at Ponsonby-Bleek's estate tomorrow. I shall reveal the killer then!"

Emotional Chaos

With that intriguing comment, Blancmange dismissed Glucose. When the Scotland Yard man had left I asked, "Surely you don't know the killer merely from what our friend Glucose has disclosed!"

He sat back in his chair with a look of deep concentration. "I shall by tomorrow, my dear Broadbeam! But for now, I must think!"

He lit another joint and sat back, closing his eyes.

"No motive and few suspects! This is indeed a three-spliff problem!"

As Blancmange had requested, Inspector Glucose summoned the solicitors Pommeroy, Wolfbane, Harker and Cohen to Sir Ponsonby-Bleek's country estate, Writhing-In-Agony, where we were to meet them, along with all the household servants. Taking the 902 from Paddington, we arrived at the brooding Sussex manor at 11:00.

"A beastly place!" I said, as the cab brought us up the driveway. "I'm surprised the murder didn't happen here!"

"The obvious choice isn't always the correct one, my dear Broadbeam!" Blancmange replied. "Do you remember 'The Case of the Chortling Corpse', as you called it in your memoirs of our adventures?"

"Quite so! Everyone assumed Leslie Boringham to be the victim of murder, simply because his severed head was found in the coal scuttle, when in fact he was the murderer!"

We were met at the door by Fatswaller, the butler. A thick set man with large mutton chop side whiskers, he seemed quite capable of a dismember murder.

"Welcome to Writhing-In-Agony, gentleman. The others are in the study!" He led us to a large, book-lined library, where Inspector Glucose had assembled everyone known to be connected to the case.

"Welcome, gentlemen! I think everyone here is familiar with the great Inspector Blancmange, and his friend and biographer,

Emotional Chaos

Colonel Sebastian Broadbeam, late of the Royal Horse Marines!"

The room was filled with a motley collection of British society. The solicitors, Mssrs. Pommeroy, Wolfbane, Harker and Cohen stood about nervously, as though being lawyers made them automatically suspect. Also in attendance were the household servants. In addition to Fatswaller, there was Smails, the groundskeeper, Mrs. Smails, the cook, Maireid, the Irish serving girl and young Moxley, Ponsonby-Bleek's personal secretary.

"Thank you for indulging me", said Blancmange, "For today, I shall reveal the perpetrator of this foul murder!"

There was an audible gasp in the room. "But how, Inspector Blancmange?" said Moxley, "all the forces of Scotland Yard have been unable solve this heinous crime!"

"I have methods unavailable to the Metropolitan police, as you will soon see. Please, everyone, take your seats. Even the servants. I don't think Sir Ponsonby-Bleek will object!"

A laugh broke the tension, and when all were seated, Blancmange said, "This was a difficult case indeed! Let me say first that I've eliminated all the servants and Mr. Moxley as suspects. As you can see from this copy of his will, which he kept framed on the wall of the study, not only didn't he leave you so much as a farthing, he gave you one week to clear off his property. As none of you stood to inherit, none had motive to kill him. Then, I thought about it... no heirs, a confiscatory estate tax... it lead me on one conclusion. The murderer was... Queen Victoria!"

Another audible gasp filled the room. "We are not amused!" said the Queen.

I jumped to my feet. "I say! When did you come in, Your Majesty?"

"We were passing by and saw that you were having a yard sale."

"And that was your undoing, Your Highness!" Blancmange said triumphantly. "During your last parade, I noticed the 'We brake for yard sales' sticker on the royal carriage. I knew that you

Emotional Chaos

wouldn't be able to resist my bait! Take her away, Glucose!"

The Queen leapt back. "You'll never take us alive!", she said, pulling a derringer from her snood. "We took out Lincoln with this, we know how to use it!"

With that she crashed through the window and ran to her carriage. Blancmange was nonplussed.

"She won't get far. I took the liberty of having Sergeant Haffwitt garrote her driver. By the time she realizes it, Glucose's men will have her surrounded!"

"Brilliant, Blancmange!" I said.

"And that's not all. If you look in the carriage, you'll find a leather apron and blood stained knives! I think we can also put the Ripper murders to rest!"

"The nation owes you a debt it can never repay, Blancmange!" said Glucose, "although I wouldn't expect a knighthood if I were you!"

THE HOUSE OF SEVEN FABLES

Everyone is familiar with Aesop's Fables, many of which have become part of our collective culture. Stories such as *The Fox and the Grapes*, *The Tortoise and the Hare*, *The Boy Who Cried Wolf* and *The Ant and the Grasshopper* are known and loved throughout the world and have taught generations many valuable lessons.

Aesop may have been the Stephen King of fables, but he wasn't the only one churning them out back in the day. There were several fabulists who plied their trade with varying degrees of success and fame. There were Pyorrhea the Greek, Polyp of Thebes, The Gaul Gall to name a few, but none save Ignavus could match the storytelling skill of Aesop. Ignavus, who lived in the Roman Province of Diphtheria between 637 and 588 BC (he was thought to have lived in Macedonia, Sarcoidosis and Mitochondria, but records from the time are sketchy. All that is known is that he was popular at parties) was known throughout the ancient world and was a favorite of King Pleistocene, a veritable Good Housekeeping Seal of Approval in the Ancient World. Anyway, who can forget such classics as:

The Slave and the Ham

A slave named Giardia stole a ham from the ham loft of his master. The master found out and had him executed.

The moral: It sucks to be a slave.

The False Gods

Word got back to Olympus that the Lymphocytes were worshiping false gods. Zeus had Gracchus, the God of Oatmeal (who was pretty low on the god list) go amongst their numbers in human form to see if it were true. While wandering through the town of Agoraphobia he was hit by a chariot, which, his being in mortal form, wasn't covered by his health insurance.

The moral: If you're going to be a god get in line early to get a good assignment, like the God of Wine or the God of Nymphomaniacs. Also, it's good to get supplemental insurance when you travel.

King Leonidas and the Wombat

This fable has been lost to antiquity, which is too bad, it sounds like it was interesting.

The moral: Always make back up copies.

The Jewish Peddler

There was once a Jewish Peddler in Rome named Mordecai the Peddler (not by coincidence; he wisely registered the name early in his career on the advice of his cousin, Menachem the Wise). Being Jewish he faced discrimination and being kosher he couldn't eat Roman delicacies such as hummingbird tongues and ocelot spleens. Outraged at the injustice of it all, he called upon Yahweh to smite Rome. But Yahweh wasn't in a smiting mood that day so he sent a rain of wine and manna, which made the Romans happy, but sticky. Feeling abandoned by Yahweh, Mordecai converted to Espicopalianism. Yahweh, not too thrilled about this, smote him mightily, turning his water into even more brackish water with those nasty little bits floating in it and his oxen into poodles.

The moral: Don't get on Yahweh's bad side.

The Man Who Would Be King

It was a time of great leaders; Mastoid of Antioch, the Roman Emperor Phallus; Sheik Alleg, leader of the Ablah Tribe; Sheena of Aleppo, sometimes called Xena, sometimes Chuck for some reason; King Turpis of Selenium... you get the point. A humble shepherd wanted to be a great king, too, so he declared himself the king of his small island and ruler off all its inhabitants. He was thought to be touched in the head so he was widely ignored, especially by his wife.

The moral: Don't be an idiot.

The Boy Who Inadvertently Cried Wolf

One day a boy named Timmius was playing near the old well when he fell in for the seventh day in a row. His loyal dog Lassius was getting pretty sick of going for help, and was busy gnawing on a ham bone she got from a slave named Giardia. So, she asked her friend the wolf to help out. When Timmius saw the wolf he cried out "Wolf! Help!" The townsfolk, who had all read *The Boy Who Cried Wolf* ignored him and he drowned. In all honesty, they were getting sick of hauling him out of the well, too, so no one saw it as a great loss.

The moral: Darwin's Law was in effect long before he was born.

The Gatekeeper and the Kraken

Catarrh, the gatekeeper of The Carpal Tunnel, would let no one pass until they answered three questions, mostly relating to his tax return. Those who failed to answer correctly had to face the Kraken. One day the Kraken got loose into the aqueduct and made an awful mess.

The moral: Krakens make lousy pets, especially if you live in a small apartment.

SCREEN PLAY

I don't think there's anyone out there who hasn't at one time or another thought about writing a screenplay that would, of course, be turned into a Hollywood blockbuster. Maybe in Tinseltown any young mechanic can be a panic (depending on his pan), but it takes effort, talent and luck to write the next Oscar winning script. But Hollywood success has it's rewards, as with Matt Damon and Ben Affleck, whose *Good Will Hunting* won multiple awards including two Oscars. On the down side it launched the acting career of Ben Affleck. The universe has a strange way of maintaining balance, wouldn't you say?

We've done some research and found the following screenplays just begging to be made. If there are any Hollywood moguls out there looking for fresh new ideas, you probably don't have much of a future as a Hollywood mogul.

Olympic

The story of *RMS Titanic*'s sister ship (official slogan: "Hey, at least we managed to cross the ocean without sinking"), from her launching in 1911 until being struck from the rolls in 1935. Since the "Star Crossed Lovers" thing has been done to death, and without the ship's sinking to add drama, it really hasn't the same glamour as *Titanic* (Jack and Rose moved to New Jersey and opened a hardware store where they lived until he died of a heart attack, after which Rose moved to Florida). So, to make it interesting they had to introduce *Olympic*'s evil twin, *Satanic* as the antagonist.

Doomed from the Start

Not a disaster flick, *Doomed from the Start*, is a romantic comedy. Envisioned as a reunion vehicle for *Gigli* stars Ben Affleck and Jennifer Lopez, the title refers to the chances of it ever being made.

Emotional Chaos

Larry Porter and the Magician's Rock

Though deemed "too derivative, even for Hollywood" they plan to make it anyway. Rather than risk legal action, the rewrite is called *A Utah Wizard in King Edward's Court*, as Mark Twain is dead and not likely to sue. It follows the adventures of a young wizard as he graduates wizard school after ten or twenty years (about the age the Harry Potter kids will be when they finally graduate in their last film, *Harry Potter and the Broken Hip*, slated for release in 2025) and goes back in time to help King Edward the Longshanks defeat William Wallace.

Platoon: The Musical

The less said about that one the better...

Mon Fromage Pathetique

Set in France in the early 1970s, it's the poignant (or pungent, depending on who you ask) story of a young, idealistic cheesemaker who yearns to make it in the big city. He moves to Paris, meets the woman of his dreams and opens a cheese shop. But, after botulism kills Jim Morrison, he becomes part of a coverup that leads to his undoing. A broken man, he returns alone to his small village and never again makes cheese.

It's Pat! II: Down Pat

Because both of the people who went to see the original demanded it! Hey, if the first one got made anything can happen, right?

Pale Writer

The inspiring tale about an albino who rejects the traditional albino occupation of assassin and instead aspires to be a journalist. He faces prejudice not only from the traditional media but threats

Emotional Chaos

from the albino community at large (being made up largely of assassins, they're well armed). He prevails, though, and goes on to become President of Fox News. Based on a true story.

Manatee

A horror movie about a giant mutant manatee that terrorizes a small Maine town. While slated for production in 2002, the project was delayed by a lawsuit from Stephen King, who claimed exclusive rights to all stories about small towns in Maine being terrorized by supernatural or mutant beings.

The Age of Disinclination

Based on the novel by either Jane Austen or Thomas Hardy this study of genteel English country life in the early 19th century would be a perfect vehicle for Kate Winslet and the guy in *Bridget Jones* who isn't Hugh Grant. Or maybe the Farrelly Brothers, just to liven things up.

The Kelp Diary

An animated family flick about life in the sea as seen through the eyes of a clump of kelp. If kelp had eyes and was cute and cuddly this baby would be in Pixar's hands before you could say "Robin Williams".

The Unnatural

The story of a young baseball player who, on his way to fame and fortune is shot by a deranged fan. He returns as a soulless zombie, and is, of course, immediately signed by the Yankees. Tasked with hitting a home run to win the big game, he instead eats the umpire's brain and the Yankees lose. Serves them right.

The Greatest Team Ever

Most people think the 1927 New York Yankees were the greatest team in baseball history, but they'd be wrong. Granted, they had the legendary "Murderer's Row": Earle Combs, Mark Koenig, Babe Ruth, Lou Gehrig, Bob Meusel and Tony Lazzeri as well as a supporting cast of talented players led by legendary manager Miller Huggins. Still, their 110-44 win-loss record was nothing compared to the now all but forgotten Cleveland Dreadnaughts of the Federal League.

In 1915 the Cleveland Dreadnaughts went 157-0, the first, last and only major league baseball team to have a perfect season. Of course, with such stars as Orbs Doweled, Rube Crowder, Moonlight Bey, Highpockets Parkhurst, Dummy Hoyle, Specs Gaffney, Charlie "The Clenched Sphincter" Tammany, Lunger Lewis, Lou "The Iron Lung" McClintock, Hans "Kraut" Himmler, Tony "Wop" Lombozzi, Moishe "Hebe" Berkowitz, Jimmy "Mick" O'Reilly, Stanley "Polack" Waslewski and, of course, their manager Lloyd "Six Toes" McGee, what else would you expect? Only Berkowitz isn't enshrined in the Hall of Fame because of his connection to the Blue Sox Scandal of 1921. Or because he was Jewish. Things were different back then.

The upstart league had raided the National and American Leagues of some of their finest talent, including Jack Quinn, Chief Bender, Edd Roush, Mordecai "Three Finger" Brown, Doc Crandall, Al Bridwell and Hal Chase as well as lesser known players such as Moose LaRue, Clyde "The Human Mystery" Krieger, Moses "Meat" Slaughter, Garters Matthewson, Chief Weaver, Doc Deacon, Farley "Death to Flying Things" Fletcher, Biscuit Pants Jennings and Cracker Holmes. By the time they started playing in 1914 some considered them a legitimate threat to the dominance of the established leagues.

The Dreadnaughts opened the 1915 season with a rollicking

Emotional Chaos

19-0 win against the Toledo Turpetude. They then beat every team they faced and with each win their following grew. Every day, in every barbershop, saloon, haberdashery, smokehouse, apothecary, sawmill, gristmill, woolen mill, sweat shop and bordello the same question was asked: will the Dreadnaughts ever lose? As the season wore on the suspense grew. Every newspaper in the country was following the team; songs and poems were written about them and every sports writer from Ring Lardner to Grantland Rice was covering them night and day. Even President Woodrow Wilson issued a proclamation that said, in part:

"As long as the Cleveland Dreadnaughts Base Ball Club continues to inspire America, I pledge to keep us out of the World War and the Negro out of Base Ball!"

But the losses never came. On and on they rolled, crushing every opponent. The closest they came to a defeat was in a game against their arch-rivals, the Chicago Stockyards. It was a blistering hot July day in Chicago, and Claude "The Invisible Man" Raines was on the mound for the Stockyards. Their infield, the combination of Jauron to Lamby to Swain (that the New York Tribune said "made 'Tinker to Evers to Chance' look like well masticated horse flesh") were making flawless play after flawless play. Tied in the twenty first inning, Stockyards manager "Pip" Longstocking decided to pull his starting pitcher for an untried rookie, "Rookie" Hobbs. In one of those stories that become a part of baseball legend, Hobbs faced the league's best batter, "Shiver" Metimbers. We'll let the Chicago World tell the story:

"Showing the demeanor and poise of a seasoned veteran, Rookie Hobbs twirled the horsehide toward Metimbers, known to one and all as 'The King of the Long Ball'. In a move that surprised no one, Metimbers knocked it over the fence and out of sight. Outraged, the spectators spilled onto the field and lynched Longstocking on the spot. His spirit as well as his rib cage crushed, Hobbs was returned to the minors."

Sadly, Hobbs never played another game in the major leagues.

Emotional Chaos

Hobbs wasn't the only player left in the wake of the juggernaut that was the Dreadnaughts. They could do no wrong that year. Every player hit over .400 and three of their pitchers won 30 games. But it wasn't to last. At the end of the season the Federal League folded and the team disbursed to the four corners of baseball.

They're all gone now, the Federal league just a footnote of baseball history. But there remains in Cleveland a plaque where Shocker Field once stood. It reads "On this spot stood Shocker Field, home of the Cleveland Dreadnaughts of the Federal League (1914-1915) and the Cleveland Tortoises of the International League (1926-62)". It may be a toxic waste dump now, but there are those who swear that if you walk past on a perfect, warm summer night you can still hear the roar of the crowds and smell the popcorn. We think it's caused by the chemical fumes.

ABOUT THE AUTHOR

Well known to all the hipsters, glitterati and bouncers in town, Brian Codagnone is a cartoonist, writer, historian, international playboy by day and crime fighter by night. He is the author of the books *Emotional Chaos*, *The Hartford Whalers*, *Hey, America! It's Misfits Time!* and co-author of *The Boston Garden* and *The Bruins in Black and White* volumes 1 and 2. He is also the creator of the comic strips *Misfits*, *S1019* and *In The Zone* as well as the humor column *Emotional Chaos*. His work can be seen at *www.corbettfeatures.com*.

www.ingramcontent.com/pod-product-compliance
Lightning Source LLC
Chambersburg PA
CBHW071005040426
42443CB00007B/679